DOG PARK WISDOM

EVERYday DOg CARE ADVICE

DOG PARK WiSDOM

EVERYday DOG CARE ADVICE

LISA WOGAN

Photography by BEV SPARKS

Fall River Press

Interior design by Mayumi Thompson

Fall River Press
122 Fifth Avenue
New York, NY 10011

ISBN: 978-1-4351-2377-9

Printed and bound in China

10 9 8 7 6 5 4 3 2 1

This book is not intended as a substitute for professional assistance, veterinary advice, or your own
good judgment. It should be used only as one of several resources in caring for and maintaining the
health of your pet. The author and publisher disclaim any responsibility for adverse effects resulting
directly or indirectly from information contained in this book.

LIVE LIFE. MAKE RIPPLES.

For Lulu, who is my daily source of dog wisdom

Contents

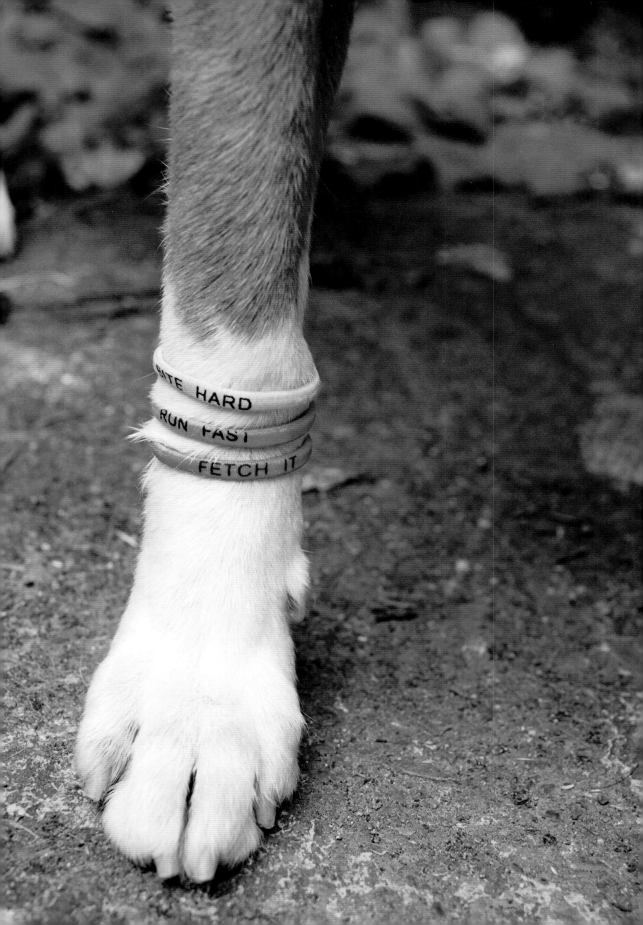

Introduction

DOG PARK WISDOM IS A BOOK OF PRACTICAL ADVICE, homespun tips, and stories—direct from the dog park—for and about living with your dog. It's a grassroots approach to pet care gleaned from everyday "dog people." I didn't seek out vets, trainers, behaviorists, or anyone else with advanced degrees or training in canine-ology. Not because they don't provide excellent counsel but because they write their own books, and let's face it, sometimes the best advice comes from a wise friend.

This book is not about studies and theory, but personal experience and trial and error. My sources are family, friends, friends of friends, and many dozens of complete strangers who have stumbled onto unorthodox and sometimes quirky insights in the course of living with dogs. Out of necessity or ingenuity, they have improvised solutions for everything from shoe chewing and barking in the car to keeping a dog cool on hot days and learning to swim. These people know how to get stains out of carpet and how to keep dogs out of the garden, always with a distinct emphasis on the doable. Leave it to busy non-pros to be reasonable in their expectations.

The idea of the dog park here is both real and metaphorical. It's not just an off-leash area. It's all parks, sidewalks, trails, fields, lakes, agility barns, training classes, confirmation rings, and homes that we share with our dogs. It also includes a vibrant, dog-centered Internet universe, which has the communal feeling of a park without the actual romping, barking, and pooping. In these environments, guardians share their rescued dog stories, confess to bad habits, complain, and give and receive advice on every possible topic from homemade snacks to fur dyes—some of which is scooped up in my net, although not the fur dyes.

What this book is not is comprehensive or systematic. How could it be with random conversations as my guide? Instead, the topics on the minds of the dog people around me, their concerns and joys, are my topics. In this way, I don't answer every possible question or address every facet of doggie life. Plus, I avoid diet, nutrition, and medical advice. It's not that these aren't priorities—they are. And folks at the dog park are certainly talking about everything from cancer in dogs to corn in diets, but addressing this sensitive advice requires context and education beyond the scope of this book.

In the last few days of writing *Dog Park Wisdom,* I made my daily trek to a local coffee shop. My dog, Lulu, was snuffling around for scone bits out front, where two women were chatting over

lattes. While I looped Lulu's leash around a post, one of the women told me about her snack-oriented beagle, who got a cookie from a bank teller one time, and for the next seventeen years always pulled toward the bank every time they passed. Clearly, I could relate. While I ordered my coffee, she walked out to her car and brought back an enormous peanut butter snack for my dog. (She offered it to me, out of Lulu's vision, which I appreciated.) I never got her name, nor she mine. But the idea that a perfect stranger would give me a gift seemed emblematic of the dog park community—generous and convivial.

This book is intended as much to recognize and celebrate that community as it is to provide concrete information. It's one reason nearly everyone who shared some tidbit with me is acknowledged at the back of the book (see "Fonts of Wisdom: Dog Park Brain Trust"). While many of my tipsters hail from Seattle and the Northwest, where I live, there are shout-outs from all around the country, with a variety of perspectives and species represented. There are a few individuals whose names were never known to me, like the man who lost his pants at the dog park (you'll have to read about it). While they can't be officially acknowledged, they are here with us in spirit. As are the experts—the trainers, behaviorists, veterinarians, and writers—whose knowledge has filtered down to us.

What constantly surprises me is that for so many of the dog people I talked to, love of an individual dog translates into love for many. Guardians with already full plates take time to reach beyond their immediate furry concerns. They help with rescues, at shelters, and in parks. They agitate for no-kill policies and legislation to end cruelty. These commitments enrich our relationships with dogs and with each other. As part of the wisdom in this book, I tell some stories of canine-oriented volunteerism and activism, with a dash of you-can-do-it-too.

In the midst of thinking about all the choices we can make to keep our dogs happy and healthy, it's important to remember the myriad things they do for us. They provide perspective, protection, loyalty, and motivation. They inspire us to try new things, even to the point of dramatically changing our lives. You'll meet several people in the coming pages—a development worker, a dog-treat baker, the inventor of the Kong, a dog day-care owner among them—for whom life was transformed through canine intervention. In these cases, the wisdom of the dog park comes not from the bipeds shuffling around with plastic bags and Wubbas, but directly from the dogs.

In the Beginning

IN THE BEGINNING, THERE WAS THE DOG. Maybe a pale, fuzzy bundle your parents brought home, or a skinny stray who moved into the garage, or a big-eyed shelter hound you finally adopted once you were on your own. From the moment that dog appeared on the scene, everyone within barking distance started learning and improvising. Eventually, those lessons, strategies, and mistakes (we all make them) were passed along to family and friends, sending more great stories and killer strategies cycling through the larger world of dog guardians.

In this chapter, I step into a life with dogs near the starting point—finding a future best friend and bringing him or her home. Next, I turn my attention to bad behaviors because, well, little challenges often come hand-in-hand with a pet license and free treats. But have no fear. From chewing to barking, a dog's natural but annoying habits fire our innovative spirits. I finish the chapter with some food fun, because from the very first day, chow is a necessity. For some dogs, it's more than that. For some dogs, peanut butter biscuits are howl-at-the-moon, big-sad-eyes, drool-dripping ecstasy.

SEVEN TRIED AND TRUE TIPS FOR CHOOSING A DOG

It's funny. If you want a baby, people don't generally volunteer advice on how to go about it (unless they're your mother). But say you want a dog, especially your first dog, and look out! The advice will flow like Vesuvius. And honestly, that's a good thing. You want to listen up. I've found that while dog people disagree about many things, when it comes to bringing home your first, second, or fifteenth dog, seasoned dogsters come together on some universal principles.

1. Identify your dog expectations.

Wendy Hughes-Jelen, a copywriter and designer in Seattle, recommends taking a breed-selector test to help you identify what you are looking for in your pet. When she decided she wanted a dog as a walking companion, she filled out an online questionnaire with responses about her lifestyle, activity level, time and grooming constraints, allergies, etc. (There are many interactive breed-selector tests online; take more than one and compare the results.) "It also helps you figure out what *your* expectations are," she says. Her top matches were Italian greyhound and corgi. Wendy adopted Sophia, the first Italian greyhound she had ever seen IRL (in real life), through rescue, and has found her to be a wonderful companion.

2. Do your research.

When New Yorker Petie Hoving fell for miniature pinschers (known among fans as min-pins) at the Westminster Kennel Club Dog Show, she didn't run out and buy one. She first read

First-dog reality check. Ask yourself: Are you even ready for a dog? Borrow a friend's dog for at least a week so you can begin to understand the daily commitment.

If you want straight talk about a particular breed, rescue folks are the people to call. They have no incentive to sell you on a dog you might not keep.

Try a hands-on experience. Before Mandy Hall in McKinney, Texas, adopted her Great Dane, Simon, she volunteered for two Great Dane rescues. "I just wanted to make sure this breed would work with my family and our lifestyle," Mandy says.

Would you consider a brown dog? Big brown or black nondescript dogs have a hard time finding homes, as do breeds with bad reputations.

Fostering a shelter or rescue dog is a way to test-drive a particular dog, or dogs in general, and help ease the pressure on shelters. Folks who end up adopting a foster dog are sometimes called "foster flops," but don't let that stop you from doing good.

a book about them and then she called the president of the Miniature Pinscher Club of America, who didn't mince words about the min-pin's downside. These are high-maintenance dogs, the president warned Petie. Dogs who not only love to burrow but who also would insist on sleeping under the covers with her. "She was right!" Petie says. Ready and eager to face these challenges, she bought a min-pin. Thirteen years and three min-pins later, she is devoted to her dogs and even started a min-pin rescue.

3. No pet stores.

Over and over, people who purchased their dogs from dog stores say they would never do it again. It's a newbie mistake. Dogs from puppy stores not only have health issues, but the breeding of dogs for stores fuels a brutal puppy-mill industry. Either contact reputable breeders through the American Kennel Club, the United Kennel Club, breed groups, trainers, or vets (and check the hell out of their references), or, better yet, adopt a dog from a shelter or rescue organization (many of which list available dogs at *www.petfinder.org*).

4. Avoid pressure cookers.

No high-pressure rescues or shelters or shops. Short hours, limited opportunities to spend time with the dogs, crowds, a free-for-all selection process—any of these fire-sale elements are inappropriate for adopting a family member with whom you'll spend many years.

5. Check under the hood.

When Mary Martin, an agility-dog fan from Yakima, Washington, and her husband went to select their Aussie puppy from a litter, they arrived an hour early and spent lots of pressure-free time with all the puppies. They had read about temperament testing, so they tried a few strategies to get to know the puppies quickly. Her husband kicked a wall to see how they reacted to the loud noise. Keeper, the dog they eventually brought home, was not afraid but curious. Exactly the reaction they were looking for. They also gently laid the puppies, one at a time, on their backs to discover which were frightened or aggressive. They also ran in front of the puppies to see if any followed. By measuring how interested the puppies were in them, Mary gleaned some idea about how likely they were to bond and how trainable they might be.

6. Try a different setting.

If you are adopting a dog from a shelter, and the dog acts docile or crazed in its kennel, ask to move him to a different setting or outside. Some dogs are transformed when they leave their kennel. Another place to meet shelter dogs is at adoption fairs or public walks. Claudine Randazzo in Flagstaff, Arizona, fell for Bo (a rottweiler–Doberman mix) at an adoption fair, where he was gregarious. If she'd met him at the shelter, she would have seen a terror.

7. Remember, it's a major commitment.
Every dog is unique. So, realize that regardless of all your research, you can't anticipate every eventuality. You're not buying a lamp. Be prepared to make the best of any tough bumps that come with your dog.

About seven years ago, my cousin Joanie Warner and her husband, Bob Mahler, rescued Chester, a honey-colored, dingolike mutt with satellite-dish ears and a mellow disposition uncommon in puppies. (That should have been their first clue.)

Shortly after bringing the slowpoke home, but well after the human–dog bond was securely in place, Chester stopped eating. Then, he started vomiting and had diarrhea. They took him to the vet. A corncob—probably from his days as a scavenging stray—was lodged in his intestines. His quiet demeanor was actually the lethargy of a dying dog. They agreed to costly, emergency surgery.

Almost immediately after the surgery, which he weathered like the survivor he was, he became a different creature altogether. Gone was the docile lapdog. In his place was a wily, tough-to-train cannonball. Over the years, Joanie and Bob dropped thousands of dollars on obedience training and boot camp, new

Don't be fooled. If a furry prospect licks you all over, it may just be your lotion or insect repellent.

Be prepared to change your mind. If you visit a shelter or rescue with a particular dog in mind, you might discover you connect with a different dog once you're there. Follow your heart.

Even if you adopt an adult dog, do it when you have free time to dedicate to the transition.

Some shelters include a few free obedience classes when you adopt.

carpet, a new mattress (which Chester peed on with their daughter still on it), even a replacement steak for the one he purloined from a neighbor's kitchen. "I guess 'buyer beware' doesn't apply when a dog is free," Joanie says. But still, buyer beware.

BRINGING RUFUS HOME

Finding your little four-legged bundle of joy is only the start. Next, you have to raise her, and those first few weeks are critical. Take the advice of those who have been around the block a few hundred times.

Take puppernity leave.
Helen Shewman, who works at a zoo in the Northwest, couldn't very well bring her new English setter puppies to work. So she took three weeks' vacation to concentrate full-time on settling them in, puppy proofing the house (a task that expands as the dogs grow), housebreaking, training, and instilling good habits. "It's a total lifestyle change," says Helen, who, when I saw her about four days in, looked as happy and exhausted as any new mom.

Sign up for doggie school.
One universal rule from the furry trenches: Take your dog to obedience training ASAP. When they are little, they look cute and manageable, but it's just a matter of time before an untrained puppy grows into an unmanageable adult. Even for veteran dog people, classes offer the chance to brush up on forgotten skills and learn new lessons. Mary Martin found that

in puppy obedience class, she discovered what sort of dog she had and began to understand him in terms of other dogs.

If you have children at home, bring them along. Carrie Comer enrolled her Brittany puppy, Katie, in a class within two weeks of bringing her home, and she found a trainer who agreed to let her two-year-old son, PJ, attend some classes. This way he, too, could learn about how to interact with their new puppy.

Money-saver tip: There is a lot of good, free advice out there. In addition to the help from your dog-smart friends, remember that ye olde library has plenty of DVDs and books on dog training.

Throw a puppy shower.

Cindy Trimble Kelly of Blue Ridge, Georgia, made sure she had a bounty of chew toys for her corgi puppies by throwing a shower when they were four weeks old. It was really an excuse to get together with friends and show off the puppies, but everyone went wild over the idea. They brought all sorts of gifts and plenty of chew toys.

Toys matter. For a new adult dog, don't wait for a party. Be prepared. When I brought Duchess (a large dog with an even larger grin) home from the shelter, I didn't have toys for her. I had food, leads, treats, a bed, bowls, a collar, and who knows what else. But I had nothing set aside for chomping or chewing. In the first four hours, before we made an emergency toy run to the store (maybe the first in history), she shredded a seat belt strap, bisected a garden hose, sheared the legs off two dining room chairs, and nearly inhaled a tennis ball.

Remember to take photos.

Take photos of your new dog. If she's a puppy, she'll grow out of the fuzzy coat, long legs, and oversized ears before you know it. If she's an adult from a shelter, take photos to record how she flourishes in her forever home. They aren't with us long enough; keep a record. If you need an excuse, how about a new-dog announcement?

Seattle dog photographer Bev Sparks (see "Dream Job: Pawparazzi") offers these darkroom-tested do's and don'ts for home shooters.

- Don't futz about trying to frame the shot. Dogs are all about action. Let it blur.
- Do overestimate the power of a treat or a toy. The goal is to make yourself fascinating to your subject. If that means enhancing your allure with a tennis ball or a stick, so be it.
- Don't turn your photo shoot into a production or get bossy with your dog.

Invest in continuing education. Even if your dog is a Canine Good Citizen, that's no reason to rest on your laurels. Teaching old dogs new tricks keeps them engaged in life and you engaged in them. From agility and Flyball to therapy work and scent tracking, there's plenty to keep you and your dog sharp and connected.

Think outside the breed. Seattleite Vikki Kauffman trained one of her poodles to herd and all four to skijor (cross-country skiing while your dogs pull you like a sled).

- Do zero in on body parts. Your dog is more than a pretty face—a wagging tail and crossed paws may someday be your favorite images.
- Don't stand around. Try new and different angles. Shoot while lying on your back or standing over your dog.
- Do get in close, especially for black dogs. Because of the way a camera's light meter works, dark dogs in the distance usually look like indistinct blobs.

DREAM JOB: PAWPARAZZI

Dog photography isn't exactly without precedent. Ever since the first daguerreotypes, dogs have been included in family portraits. Before that, artists were commissioned to paint elegant renderings of pets, hunting companions, and farm animals alone or with their people. Today, though, professional dog portraits are almost de rigueur, like school photos for kids—which is great for a generation of talented photographers who don't mind getting dirty or even bit.

Seattle-based photographer Bev Sparks was early in the wave of dog shooters. After more than ten years photographing dogs practically full-time, she knows how to get her furry models to deliver. The results are mostly black-and-white, documentary-style portraits that testify to each dog's particular *je ne sais quoi*.

Bev's secret could be that, at fifty-four, she's as eager to play in the dirt as a puppy, yet she's as patient and crafty as an old stray. That means during a one- to two-hour photo session, on her subjects' home turf, she manages to capture a dog's infinite variety from wild abandon to sweet repose—and all the shades in between. It's terribly satisfying for people who have spent years mentally cataloging their dogs' many moods.

Her signature is probably images of "dog parts," close-ups of dog anatomy. By paying careful attention to the crook of a leg, a stubby tail, or a wet ear, she discovers unsung beauty and often humor.

Bev darts around town in a PT Cruiser, wearing black high-top Converse sneakers and a pouch filled with treats. In her pocket, she carries a squeaker from an old toy. She's photographed hundreds of dogs, plus cats, rats, mice, rabbits, horses, and cockatiels.

Although she's been a professional photographer for more than twenty-five years, she hit on the dog angle by accident. She didn't even have a dog at the time. While taking classes toward a BFA, she got the assignment to photograph a single object in as many ways as she could find. Her "object" was a rust-colored mutt named Roy. When she hung that homework in a pet shop, she landed commissions. Today, she is so busy through word-of-mouth (especially after an appearance on *Oprah*) that she's nearly phased out non-dog work.

She has published her photos in several books and has a line of her own greeting cards and magnets. For several years, her calendars have helped raise money for local shelters.

But professional success is a by-product for Bev. "If I haven't photographed dogs for awhile, it's like my heart's been closed," she says. "When I get back to it, I realize how much I miss them. It's like the sun comes out."

Second Dogs

Tasselhoff Burfoot, a basset hound with soulful eyes, was an only pup when Mary Mischelle Kemp brought another basset, Fizban, into her Utah home. That event earned her the silent treatment for three months. When Mary went to pet Tas, he'd walk away. When she had guests, he'd go up to them and let them pet him while he stared down Mary. Mary's mom, who is not into dogs, told her daughter, "*That* dog is mad at you."

If you do get a second dog, reinforcements help. When Joshua Madsen added an Australian shepherd puppy to his one-schnauzer household in Orlando, he was happy his new girlfriend was eager to help with love and attention 24/7.

Introduce the two dogs in neutral territory. As Joshua points out, "neutral" means avoiding not just home and backyard, but also your dog park or other regular stomping grounds. In addition, don't try to force them to be best friends. Just create a positive, consistent environment.

If you have more than one dog, don't be afraid to leave one of them behind sometimes. Matt Cohn says he's learned it's good for Rosie and Hazel to have alone time.

"But what are you going to do?" Mary asks. She'd made a lifelong commitment to Fiz just like she had to Tas. "When I get my puppies, I hold them in my hand and promise them I'll take care of them for the rest of their lives." Finally she just told Tas, "He's here now."

Perspectives on second dogs are as varied as the dogs themselves. Sometimes a new dog is welcome. Peggy Sherman, who has headed up a multi-pet family in Madison County, Florida, for more than thirty years, says her beagle was visibly relieved when a new dog took over leadership of the pack. Matt Cohn, an attorney and woodworker in Boulder, got his puppy Rosie (a black Lab mix) with the hopes she might grow into a sort of guide buddy for Hazel, a flat-coated black Lab–golden retriever mix, who had lost 70 percent of her vision due to retinal dysplasia. Rosie is still a puppy, but already she breaks the ice with new people for her nearly blind pack mate.

I know one couple who consistently add a second dog to the household when the original dog seems just about ready to go. They refer to the new addition as the overlap dog. Of course, the dog who is being overlapped doesn't always head straight for the Rainbow Bridge. When Judy Trockel's beagle turned sixteen, she got a second dog to eventually take his place. Boogie is now nineteen-and-a-half and still walks a mile a day in his Redmond, Washington, off-leash area.

Other folks won't go there. One man told me he'd never get a second dog while his current dog was alive. "It's like taking a mistress," he said.

THE NAME GAME

I spend too much time coming up with names for dogs that aren't mine. I want a pair of corgis, which I'll name Madeleine Albright and Butros Butros Gali. I like the name Snack for a little dog and Trifle for a mastiff. But when I adopted Lulu, I froze up. I couldn't come up with a name for weeks. Finally, one of my co-workers suggested Tallulah Bankhead, and out of desperation I named my dog after a promiscuous, hard-drinking, pill-popping actress. You want to be prepared.

The first rule, as they say, is there are no rules. But there are some guidelines.

- Keep names short.
- Test drive names by hollering them out the front door.
- Try not to pick names that sound like commands—Chum, Ray, Zit, etc.
- If you have more than one dog, try to keep the names distinct from one another.

Try Kermit, Abercrombie, Zooma.
Have a field day. You don't have to worry about other dogs teasing them for a silly name.

Avoid Max, Jake, Buddy, Maggie, Molly, Lady.
If you plan on socializing, hitting day cares and dog parks, you'll want to avoid the more popular dog names such as Max and Maggie. There are a dizzying number of Lucys at my dog park. You can make a list of names to avoid by checking the online archive of your city paper. There are often annual stories about pet license registrations that include lists of the most popular dog names. There are also websites using this information to sell pet tags.

Lots of folks teach their dogs to come to a whistle. There are a few advantages to this. First of all, it's cool. Second, some people can whistle louder than they can yell. Third, if your dog is an escape artist, it's less embarrassing—and traceable— to whistle for your dog at two in the morning as opposed to yelling *Klondike*!

Consider Holly, Ginger, Sienna.

Carol Beebee of Placerville, California, prefers naming her pets after things—plants, herbs, colors. Her photographer husband, Martin, prefers people names. So they find compromises that work for both.

What about Blackie, Lady Wiggles, and Miss Daisy One Dot?

Following a Native American tradition, Dave Swenson named his rat terrier for a physical characteristic—in Miss Daisy One Dot's case, a dot on her rear. The choice of Daisy was alliterative. "I wanted a dog with a name that you could swear at easily," Swenson says, which was prescient since she engineered many frustrating escapes during their early days together. On the way home from the shelter, she made her first mad dash out the car door across the Iowa plains. Dave found her in a mobile home park, and originally dubbed her Tanya Trailer Trash.

Have a name in reserve.

People almost always decide what their offspring will be called before seeing them or getting to know them. Why not do the same for a dog? Phil Juliano always knew he'd

name his dog Spencer, after the savvy private detective in Robert B. Parker novels (although where Parker spelled it with an *s*, Phil uses a *c*). The advantage to this advance decision is that from the moment the five-week-old Lab plopped his butt onto Phil's fiancé's feet—making the selection a no-brainer—they called him Spencer. The mocha-colored pup stayed behind for a few more weeks with his littermates and mom, with the breeder calling him Spencer the entire time. When Phil brought him home, the puppy knew his name.

If you think you've heard of a Lab named Spencer, it may be because you've seen Phil's comic strip *Best in Show,* which chronicles—and embellishes—the travails of a coffee-loving baseball fan and his silly, sarcastic, and

culturally plugged-in pup. While Phil uses pseudonyms for real world–inspired humans in his strip, Spencer is just Spencer on the assumption that his dog won't sue him.

BREAKING BAD HABITS

Most training wisdom comes down to us from skilled and articulate professionals—gifted trainers and behaviorists who work magic with the hardest cases. Responsible guardians take their dogs to obedience classes, participate in other training, and read books, and then they apply that experience to their own situations. They sift expert advice through the cheesecloth of daily life, sometimes in contradiction of the pros. Their best ideas aren't strategies that *sound* good or work in *some cases*; their best ideas are those that worked in the most important case, their own.

Peeing Indoors

Say "puppy." Some people will think fuzzy, sweet-smelling cuddle-balls romping in tall grass. The stuff of Hallmark cards. But anyone who knows anything will envision urine stains and destruction.

Cindy in Georgia house-trained her corgis by the time they were seven weeks old, so she knows something. The key to her approach was keeping an eye on them: Whenever they looked anxious, she put them outside. If they did any business, she followed up with positive encouragement. At night, they slept in crates. Because they don't like to mess where they sleep, they let Cindy know when they needed to go outside, for which they were richly rewarded.

Because she owns her own company, she was able to bring the dogs to work, which made monitoring them in a free-standing, collapsible indoor pen easy. To introduce them to peeing outdoors, she started them on paper in the pen. They were first rewarded for doing their business there. (She has jars of small cookies all over her office, so she can reward good behavior swiftly.) Once they were trained to paper, Cindy moved the "play area" and the paper closer and closer to the outdoors, until finally the paper was outside and then it was gone.

Puppies aren't the only dogs to need help with housebreaking. Shelter dogs, foster dogs, outdoor dogs, and just your basic backsliders can require a refresher. Sometimes bringing a new puppy into the house will cause an older, trained dog to regress. They will smell the scent from the puppy's accidents, and think "Woo-hoo, rules have changed. I can pee inside now."

If you can't take your new dog to work to monitor the house-training process there, remember pupternity leave, also known as vacation.

Don't leave water out all the time. When you do, monitor your puppy's drinking and be sure she gets breaks within a half hour. Best not to let her drink before bed.

Many of the same techniques that work for puppies, especially monitoring water and behavior at all times, apply. Sometimes, though, chronic indoor accidents may be the sign of a physical problem, so check with your vet.

How to make a stay-on diaper.

Incontinence caused by a variety of long- and short-term health problems is another challenge. When diapers are needed, it can be hard to keep them on your dog. Clevelander Nicole Gendics had a boxer named Arnold who had to wear diapers due to kidney problems. Unfortunately, he would rub them against the wall until they came off. She sewed a pair of boxer shorts to a tank top to create a jumper to hold the diapers in place. After that, he wore them without problems.

PETS FOR YOUR PET

There's this idea that dog people don't like cats (and vice versa). I don't think it's true. In fact, dog people and dogs tend to like a lot of different critters under the right circumstances. (And I don't mean "like" in a stalking-from-the-window sort of way.) Cats, rabbits, rats, mice, guinea pigs, parrots, and many other pets have all been man's best friend's best friend—often with surprising results.

Lynn T.'s Newfoundland lived for several years with little or no use of her back legs due to a spinal compression. Lynn wanted Nell to have a buddy but worried a fully functioning quadruped would make a potentially frustrating match. A friend came up with a solution. She gave Lynn (and Nell) a fearless dwarf bunny.

Things didn't start out too well. The bunny wasn't fixed, and he attached himself to Nell's leg, humping her constantly. After a few weeks, Lynn despaired about the friendship, and Nell seemed to be reaching her limit as well.

Then it happened. Nell's lip curled, she growled, and chomped the bunny. Lynn scrambled. There was no sign of blood, injury, or even trauma. Yet from that point forward, the bunny never humped Nell again. He'd snuggle up with her on the bed, and she'd give him a little lick. Nell died one month after her bunny died.

Linda Heidt was sharing her Pensacola home with four ferrets when she brought Scooby Doo, a rat terrier puppy, home. From day one, he loved tearing after the ferrets, who have free range of the house during the day when Linda is home. The oldest ferret, Sable, is the queen of the house, and she goes after Scooby if he bothers her too much.

One day when Linda was sorting laundry, Scooby came running up the stairs, crying and whining Lassie-like. She had just let him out, so she initially ignored him. But he kept up his desperate whining. She decided to let him outside again. He tore down the stairs. "When I got down there, I expected to find him by the door waiting to go out. Instead he was sitting in the hall facing toward the kitchen, just staring," she says. There was Sable with a piece of dog food lodged in the back of her mouth, blocking her airway. "She was just about to the point of passing out. I scooped her up and dislodged the food," Linda says, "and she was fine—not happy I took food from her—but OK. I was totally amazed that Scooby cared enough about her to get my attention."

Chewing

It's natural for dogs to chew. They chew when they're teething, investigating the world, and scavenging for food. They also chew when they are anxious or bored. Savvy dog owners know how to channel that natural impulse away from the shoe collection toward objects that will benefit canine teeth and gums.

Give them something to chew on.
Puppies are the most avid chewers. Tempt them with something tasty that will also feel good in their young mouths. Cindy's corgi puppies went crazy for a homemade, gum-soothing toy—old, clean washcloths soaked in broth and frozen.

For dogs of all ages, you can find chew toys in every shape, color, material, and price range. Favorite toys for destructive chewers include the following:

- Extra-tough rubber bones, balls, and rope toys, such as those made by Kong, TireBiter, and Hardcore
- Edible chews, such as Greenies
- Dried bull's penis (not for the faint hearted or vegetarian), such as Bully Sticks
- Durable chews made of nylon, such as bones and knots made by Nylabone

With any new chew toy, observe your dog the first few times he or she plays with it. (The instructions will tell you to watch them "always," but how realistic is that?) Make sure your dog can't break off chunks that might choke him.

Don't mortgage the farm for dog toys.
Store-bought toys are not for every dog. Buy a forty-dollar stuffed hedgehog, and your pup will prefer a worm-eaten stick or scrap of PVC pipe. Some budget-minded guardians follow that humble lead to save money. Here are a few ideas for toys that will entertain your dog without draining your wallet:

- *A sock that squeaks.* When a sock mate passes on, roll the widow into a ball or tie it off like a bow for tug-of-war. Dog photographer Bev Sparks likes to put a squeaky ball in the sock, so it's easier to throw and because her dogs prefer to "kill" something that shakes and squeaks.
- *Rockin' rolls.* Empty toilet paper rolls and paper towel rolls are a down-and-dirty good time for a short while. Of course, there's a clean-up factor. Some people amp up the frenzy by freezing a little peanut butter inside the roll.
- *Happy trails.* A trail of unsalted, unbuttered popcorn snaking through the house is an entertaining snack on a rainy day.

Beyond just looking for hardy toys, Nicole Gendics suggests teaching pups to be nice to their playthings. "It worked wonders for my dog and my wallet," she says. "I supervise him with his toys and when he turns into Mr. Destructo, I tell him 'be nice' or 'easy' or 'gentle' and take the toy away for ten minutes. If you do this each time, a dog will soon learn that ripping the crud out of his toys only gets them taken away."

■ *Chilly chompers.* Ice cubes are the ultimate cheap thrill when it's hot.

Take preventative measures.
When toys are not enough to distract a dog, guardians learn to hide their slippers. Others get inventive about dissuading mouthy canines.

Pepper your shoes. Doina Berndt's dog Maya was a bad mouther and chewer of shoes, a tough problem for two reasons. One, the Lurcher loved the taste of Doina's Bitter Apple spray, so she would lick up every drop. Two, true to her Oklahoma-on-the-border-with-Texas roots, she adored spicy food, so hot pepper was out of the question. "What finally worked was ground black pepper, because she would first sniff, inhale it, and start sneezing," Doina says. "Finally, my shoes were safe."

Shake them off. When Jeff Jablow's dogs were young, he kept a plastic soda bottle with rocks in the bottom close by. Whenever the dogs got near an electric cord or something that he just couldn't hide away, he would shake the bottle or bang it on a table to scare them off.

Tackling the Terrible Teens

Crank it up during the teen years. Carrie Comer in Page County, Virginia, stepped up training when her Brittany, Katie, hit her teen phase. Carrie introduced new tricks, more play time to burn energy, and more "puppy push-ups" (going from sit, to down and wait, and back to sit). She mixes up the length of time Katie holds a wait or a sit, so the dog has to focus on Carrie to get the next cue. Plus, she whispers, so Katie has to listen attentively, and she mixes hand cues with verbal cues to hone Katie's focus even more.

Keeping Katie on track has made Carrie a better parent in a way. "Katie reminds me that, no matter how much you love someone, you still have to have rules and guidelines to keep things happy," Carrie says. "I have a feeling that if I didn't have Katie, I'd be more tempted to let my son PJ get away with things."

Peggy Sherman in Orlando calls the teen years a tricky time. "Every dog, no matter what size or breed, reaches a point in his or her 'adolescence' when they must start to find their place in the pack, which includes their human owners," she says.

For Peggy, the transition came down to a crossroads in the living room. Rufus, her Staffordshire bull terrier, wanted domain over Peggy's chair, growling at her when she approached. "I made brief eye contact with him—enough to establish my lack of fear, but not enough to be a challenge," she says. Then she grabbed his collar and gently but firmly pulled him off the chair, saying in a confident but not overly loud voice, "Out. You are going out now."

His response was immediate, she says. His growling stopped and he went docilely out the door. That was more than four years ago. "It seems very evident to me that he likes knowing who

is in charge in this house and where his place is," she says. "So if I were to give one piece of advice to dog owners, it would be to prepare for that test, because it is as inevitable as the one that every fourteen-year-old child attempts. It might be just a strong wind that blows through or it could be a major storm."

Carrie Comer credits a lot of her two-year-old son's excellent social skills to their dog, Katie. "She never tried to guess his meaning if he screamed or pointed to something," Carrie says. "He knows he has to tell her what he wants, and that he has to play nice with Katie."

Poop Eating

There are lots of cultural and dietary theories about *coprophagia*—that's fancy Greek for eating feces. It's pretty interesting stuff, actually. What matters, though, is that if you love kissy-face, this habit is off-putting. Before you go sprinkling chili flakes on the poop or adding meat tenderizer, canned pumpkin, or spinach to dog food (some of the down-and-dirty suggestions for making turds inedible, like they aren't already), try to figure out why he or she is doing it. Something missing in the diet? Bored? Needs more exercise? If everything is hunky dory on these fronts, the best solution appears to be keeping poop-eaters away from temptation. In the yard, pick up waste immediately. When you walk your dog on-leash, keep an eagle-eye out for lone appetizers. If you have a cat, be sure the litter box is out of reach.

Use your leverage. Seattle author Michelle Goodman can get her dog, Buddy, to do *anything* right before a meal, including lying down for twenty minutes next to his full bowl.

Barking

One fix for undesirable barking is the old spray bottle. A spritz can often quiet a barking dog. But beware the law of unintended consequences. My sister Whitney used a soggy zapper to train her dog, Zipper (a sheltie–Aussie mix), to stop barking. It worked, and eventually the mere sight of the water bottle was enough to curb the noisy habit. But there is a new problem. Now that Zipper no longer barks, she no longer "uses her words" to be let out back to relieve herself. Hence she relieves herself indoors. Not a desired result.

Whitney might want to follow the example of Anne Croghan, who lives in my neighborhood in Seattle. Using treats, she trained her beagles, Amos and Oliver, to ring a bell in the kitchen when they want to go out back. It worked like a charm. But remember the law of unintended consequences? When Amos and Oliver learned that nudging the bell resulted in a treat, they developed the habit of ringing for the treat itself.

Jumping on Guests

There is no easy fix for jumping, and whatever you try will require consistency. The advice falls into two camps. Camp One: Step back. When your dog jumps on you—especially when you arrive home—ignore her, turn away, or walk away. Don't engage. When she is calm, sitting or lying down, go to her, reward and praise her, and say your hellos. Camp Two: Step in. When your dog jumps on you, move into her, pushing her back and making her uncomfortable. Some

A bathtub is often a comforting location. During storms or fireworks, dog photographer Bev Sparks puts Benny's bed in the tub, so the white shepherd mix can be cozy while he hides out. Some dogs prefer a denlike hiding place. If so, be sure there's a go-to cubby wherever you are.

Some tipsters claim slipping a snug T-shirt on a dog quells anxiety.

folks hang onto their dog until well past the moment he or she wants to get down. A final strategy is to train the heck out of "sit," so that when you need it, your dog delivers.

Kate Rogers's husky–Lab mix, Denali, was terrible about over-rambunctious greetings—jumping, howling, and whining. So the Seattle editor started to encourage her to "get your bone" (or toy). Finding a bone and holding it in her mouth calmed Denali down to a mere wiggle, which allowed guests and the pizza delivery guy easier entry.

A note about "underminers": These are those guests who say, "Oh, I don't mind your dog jumping on my white linen dress with her muddy paws," or worse, your significant other who likes the full-contact greeting and encourages it. Wise guardians know underminers need training, too.

Freaking Out

When Shelby was rescued from life in a crate, her collar had grown into her neck and she was afraid of many things, including loud noises, brooms, bags, waving arms—countless everyday objects and experiences. It was so bad her guardian, Nicole Gendics, sought the help of a behaviorist.

The fix was slow and involved. "What we did was desensitize her to one thing at a time," Nicole explains. For example, brooms. Nicole would sit and wrestle or play toys with Shelby, while someone swept the floor in the other room. Then she would repeat the routine while someone swept in the same room. Eventually, she was able to coax Shelby to the broom if it was still, and finally to sweep around her. "It sounds simple, and it was. It was just a very long process," Nicole says.

For dogs who are afraid of thunder or fireworks, some people swear by using storm recordings. They introduce their dogs to the sound of a storm, playing quietly, while the dog is doing something she enjoys. Gradually, they increase the sound (over days, not minutes), always with a positive experience associated with the sounds, until the dog associates the rumble of thunder with something fun. When the storm hits, they play with the dog to reinforce the pleasure factor. (I don't mean rewarding your dog with treats and cuddles if she acts anxious in a storm. That, apparently, only reinforces the anxiety.)

Garbage Raiders

This can be a tough habit to train your dog out of since it generally happens while the taskmaster is away from home. Sometimes it's just easier to secure the can. For height-disabled dogs, extra weight in the bottom of the can may solve the problem. One couple said baiting the "garbage" with raw hamburger meat laced with red pepper sauce put an end to the habit. There are pet-proof garbage cans on the market, but where's the challenge in that?

While You're Away

Nothing beats real interaction. And while walkers and day cares try to fill the gap, they can be expensive. Suss out your network. Maybe a dogless neighbor wants a lunch-time walking companion. I know several people who have concocted free dog-sitting arrangements. Some guardians swap dog pals back and forth depending on who is at home or who has free time, or a stay-at-home mom dog-sits in exchange for night-time babysitting.

A hollow chew toy stuffed with a tasty treat has long been a staple for entertaining dogs left at home. Treat-dispensing balls and other toys also keep pups happily engaged long after you've left the building.

Some people hide treats and toys around the house; others swear by TV or radio. There is even a crate being developed that allows a guardian at a remote location to watch his dog via webcam and dispense toys or treats with a keystroke.

Matt Cohn used to leave his mature dogs in a dog-proofed woodshop while he was at work. In addition to visits by a dog walker, he added variety to their day with a Rube Goldberg–style automatic dog-door opener. He attached one end of twine to a nail stopper holding the dog-door closed and the other end to an electric orange juicer, which was set to juice on a timer. When the timer triggered the juicer, the twine wound slowly around the cone like a spindle, pulling out a nail stopper and opening the dog door for backyard play.

Three Sensible Reminders

We all have friends who seem to have a gift for communing with canines. It's not so much how they respond to a specific circumstance as their general demeanor around dogs. They just get it. Here are three easy-to-remember strategies that go a long way toward keeping humans and dogs on a happy track together.

1. Treat them right and they'll behave.

Everyone tells Boulder photographer Robert Troup that his four Border collies are so sweet. Then they ask: How do you do that? He thinks it's because he brings them everywhere and includes them in everything he does. "They are never home alone. They're always with me. We have an agreement where I bring them out to places that they want to be, wild places where they can be dogs and run around, but they have to follow the rules when we're home and when I have to do my stuff," Troup says. "It's this agreement that works out. We both get what we need as long as we both give each other what we need. They know that they are going to be treated right. They don't have to do anything deviant or beg for anything."

Fear of people? After living on the streets of Baja, Mexico, Alley, a German shepherd mix puppy, was frightened by people, especially women. So when Daiva Gedgaudas adopted Alley, she helped the dog overcome her fear with a simple trick: Everyone who visits the Gedgaudas household comes armed with a treat for Alley.

2. Be patient.

Claudine Randazzo, who has volunteered at shelters, knew she had to be especially patient with Bo, a rottweiler–Doberman cross she adopted when he was five. He'd been in and out of shelters for so long—several years—he suffered from something called "shelter shock," when some shelter dogs lose their spark. "We were really committed to adopting adult dogs," she says. "We were fine with whatever transition he needed."

3. Forget about perfection.

Carrie Comer managed a toddler and a Brittany puppy with this approach: "Don't strive for perfect dog behavior," she says. "I go for a good dog that our family can live with."

THE KING BEHIND THE KONG

In 1970, Joe Markham faced a vexing problem. Fritz, a German shepherd he'd adopted, developed the tooth-destroying habit of chewing on rocks. By three years old, the former police dog had seriously ground down his choppers.

Joe searched far and wide for a toy to distract his prized dog from this behavior. "Fritz either didn't like them or tore them up," he says. The alternative Fritz appropriated was hardly an improvement: a motorcycle tire. He liked to run up and down the aisles of the parts department in a Yamaha dealership that Joe co-owned, banging the tire off the walls.

One day, Fritz purloined a Volkswagen bus part from a box underneath a workbench at Joe's parents' garage. It was a rubber snubber used to keep the suspension from hitting the bus frame. Joe threw it like a ball and then looked on in wonder. "Fritz didn't want his rock!" says Joe, who lives in Colorado. "He wanted this gizmo." The rest, as they say, is dog-toy history.

Friends noticed how Fritz adored the beehive shaped car part. When Joe told the story about how it helped the dog kick his rock habit, some even offered to invest in the making and selling of a similar toy. Joe took some convincing. Remember, this was back in the day before pet superstores.

Still, Joe suspected he was on to something. He applied his mechanical skills to modify the original, which was too heavy and not nearly bouncy enough. Calling it the Amazing Beetle, because it was modeled on a VW part, he shopped it around to pet stores. He got the cold shoulder.

When someone suggested it looked like an earplug for King Kong, Joe told him, "It is. It's the amazing Kong."

Even with a new name, the Kong wasn't an overnight success. A 1976 ad in Colorado regional editions of *TV Guide* yielded only 200 orders. And once Kong developed a following, the company faced challenges building the brand and dealing with knockoffs. Joe couldn't quit his day job until 1986.

Today, Kong is probably the most recommended dog toy in the world. Joe figures they've sold about one Kong for every dog in America (sometimes estimated at more than 50 million). Joe is proudest of how Kongs provide solutions for problems faced by most dog owners. For example, when Kong chew toys are filled with peanut butter or some other treat, they provide a great distraction for dogs left at home alone. The company donates imperfect Kong products to shelters, which might help some dogs become more adoptable.

More than twenty years since Joe's epiphany, Fritz is no longer with us. But Joe's current muse, Miss Trixie, still comes to work some days. The 105-dog-years-old Aussie-cross doesn't play with Kongs anymore, but she does eat the tasty stuffings. "She's our palate tester. She's really finicky," Joe says. "If you get it past Trixie, everybody here claps."

KITCHEN CONFIDENTIAL

No tapping into the word-of-mouth wisdom of dog people can exclude a mention of the largest pet-food recall in U.S. history in the spring of 2007. Pet-food ingredients contaminated by melamine, a chemical added by manufacturers in China to make the ingredients seem more protein-rich, killed thousands of cats and dogs. An exact number will never be known. In the aftermath, concerns about the quality of pet food, the lack of oversight and forthright communication, and reports of tainted products continue to ripple through the community of guardians.

At the peak of the recall, the grassroots groups took over. At veterinarian clinics, dog runs, pet food shops, dog parks, bookstores, libraries, and online chat rooms and websites, people educated themselves about what their dogs were eating. They investigated what happened, offered support to grieving and worried guardians, and then planned for what to do next.

Bloggers dedicated to companion-animal issues became a go-to choice for keeping up to date. Sites such as *www.PetFoodTracker.com* and *www.ThePetFoodList.com* became important clearinghouses for the latest news. Alternatives such as raw food, home-cooking, even vegan diets moved into the kibble-and-canned-food-dominated mainstream. People worked together for the animals.

This revolution didn't happen in a vacuum. Earlier recalls and the interest in healthy eating for humans had already trickled down to the furry omnivores at our feet. A large body of smart-eating wisdom is out there for anyone who wants it. For my purposes, I stay away from recommending specific diets and meal plans. There are just too many variables and too big a chance that as nonexperts (myself included), we'll steer you in a direction that may not be best for you or your dog. Like our own dining habits, out pets' diets should be based on their individual needs. This one-food-doesn't-fit-all realization may be the best result of our heightened awareness about dog and cat food. It's more than keeping our pups' engines running. It can be a way to address issues such as itchy skin, runny eyes, mood, and gastrointestinal problems. When it comes to making changes in your dog's diet, educate yourself and consult with your dog's health care giver. The great news is there's a whole lot of help out there.

With all those caveats, I still can't resist passing along a few food-related suggestions and ideas that seemed too yummy or smart or quirky to ignore.

Thinking about what our dogs need to be healthy, happy, and shiny can lead to better thinking about our human diets.

Despite Appearances . . .

. . . dogs can't eat everything. When their adorable French bulldog, Omar, lost the strength in his back legs and keeled over, Seattleites Dean and Kathy Schultz didn't know what the problem could be. They rushed Omar to their vet. An enema revealed macadamia nuts in his stool. They flashed on the empty macadamia nut dish back in their living room, and were shocked to discover the tasty treat could be toxic to dogs. Omar recovered quickly, but Kathy wondered what else she didn't know. Since then, she's done her research and made a list (posted on the fridge) of foods that can harm Omar and his best pal, Sophie. Sites such as *www.aspca.org* are a good place to start. The list is surprisingly long and includes, but is not limited to, chocolate, grapes, coffee, and onions.

Make snacks at home.

You can't swing a rope toy without hitting a dog bakery these days. Although bakeries make excellent walking destinations, most homes have the ingredients for plenty of tasty snacks. Here are a few homemade favorites from the dog park:

Pup-friendly popsicles. In an ice-cube tray, freeze low-sodium chicken broth or a piece of kibble in water. You'll have great refreshments for hot days.

Doggie daiquiris. When you start freezing treats, the world is your oyster. Use small paper cups or cupcake holders in a muffin pan and fill them with some combination of plain, organic low-fat yogurt, peanut butter, chicken broth, smashed bananas, papaya (supposedly good for bad breath), Iams Savory Sauce, and on and on.

Liver jerky. "Stinks up the kitchen like no other, but it's an 'instant-recall' treat," says Haley Poulos, who makes it for her hiking and backpacking companion, Charlotte. "She'll do anything for it." The Silverdale, Washington, resident is like many folks who buy food dehydrators to transform beef, chicken, and fish into tasty jerky-like snacks.

Do-it-yourself biscuits. Dog cookies are no more difficult to make than people cookies, you just have to know what ingredients to avoid (see "Despite Appearances . . .").

Carrots. These are a huge favorite. Bay Area resident George Gadda had an Akita, Pacino, who loved carrots. "He'd sit with it between his paws and chew it all the way down," George says. He also loved bananas, cherries, and blackberries, as well as bones from the butcher. "The day I had to put him down, I'll tell you what: His teeth were as white and clean as a three-year-old dog."

For Briana Solovitz's pug, Miguel Raoul, only baby carrots will do. No shredded or sliced carrots. Everytime Briana goes to the fridge to get a carrot for her guinea pig, Lil Girl, Miguel camps out next to her cage to snag one himself.

Anything with peanut butter. A Fig Newton covered with peanut butter is Miss Daisy One Dot's favorite treat. "She loves it, but it takes her a week to eat it," says guardian Dave Swenson, who loves to watch his rat terrier give it her best.

Fool chubby appetites.

Low-sodium, canned green beans bulk up the meal without adding too many calories, and French cut beans mix well with the kibble.

Entice finicky eaters and drinkers.

There are some finicky dogs out there—which amazes me. The same dogs who eat everything from a full diaper and cat poop to cockroaches, worms, and their own vomit have to be hand-fed special diets. But folks with picky eaters know how to get the job done.

If you're making homemade dog treats, and you want them extra hard, here's a trick from a savvy dog baker. When the treats are done cooking, remove the cookie sheet and turn off the oven. After a few minutes, while the oven is still warm, put the cookie sheet back in and let the treats sit overnight. They'll be crunchy-crunchy, but not burned, by morning.

Are you feeding your dog near the trash? Dogs have sensitive noses and might be put off by stinky garbage you don't even notice.

No dog can resist a little duck fat. Of course, that's not always easy to get. Seattle-based editor Kate Rogers drizzles liquid from a just-opened tuna fish can over dry kibble. For her dog Gleason, she used the packed-in-oil variety to help with his arthritis. For her dog Denali, she stuck with the packed-in-spring-water version. She would drain the liquid into a small jar and keep it in the refrigerator, using a teaspoon or so at a time on the kibble. Other appetite-enhancing sprinkle suggestions include Parmesan cheese, oregano, and low-sodium broth.

If your dog won't drink his or her water, be sure it's clean and fresh. "Every time I feed my dog, I refresh his water bowl with cool, crisp water," George Gadda says. "I've seen people fill a water bowl and leave it out there—and wait a couple days before they change it. Would you want to drink out of a water bowl that's starting to get algae in it?" If your buddy snubs fresh water, a little meat or broth baiting the water can be helpful.

Tummy Trouble

Does your dog suffer from upset tummy, constipation, and/or diarrhea? A lot of folks out there strongly advocate canned pumpkin as the remedy for such ills.

Jars of baby food (chicken or beef) with white rice and boiled chicken breast is what helped Seattleite Taresa D. soothe her beagle's sensitive stomach. Her newest pup gets organic sweet potato and apple baby food poured into a hollow chew toy and then frozen to ease teething pain.

Kevin N. in Prescott, Arizona, found that his dog Abigail Grace experienced less "windy-ness" after he put her on a consistent diet of premium food. In the case of this one-year-old malamute–Lab mix, it's large-breed puppy food. Kevin also thinks carrots helped, as well as keeping Abby clear of nonfood snacks such as tissues and cotton swabs.

JUST WHAT THE DOCTOR BAKED

You spend four years in college, four more in med school, several more sleep-deprived years completing an internship and a residency. You've arrived. You're a doctor. But you're not entirely satisfied. Then one day, while baking cookies for your adorable sheltie, you have an epiphany. You're as happy as you can remember being for a very long time. You call your parents to tell them the good news: You plan to quit medicine to bake.

This is pretty much the story of Geri Sim, a neurologist turned bakery supervisor and baker of dog-treats-for-hobby venture, the Honeybark Bakery in New Hyde Park, New York. At first, her parents thought she was a little crazy. They urged her to take a year off and reminded her she could always go back to being a neurologist. "They've long since stopped saying that because they now see how important the Honeybark Bakery is to me and how my life has changed for the better," Geri says.

Not only is she much happier surrounded by mixing bowls, cookie sheets, and Katie, her number-one taste tester, but she's also actually lost more than thirty pounds since she started full-time in the kitchen. "The baking isn't really a sidetrack from medicine, as much as medicine was a sidetrack from baking," she says.

In her dog biscuits, Geri uses all human-grade ingredients, including organic whole-wheat flour, fresh fruits and vegetables, carob (as an alternative to chocolate), breath-freshening boosts of apples and parsley, and no chemical additives. Her frosting is especially delicious—with cream cheese, cinnamon, vanilla, and honey. She likes the health benefits of honey and not having to worry about brushing Katie's teeth after she eats treats.

While Geri is not about to make creating dog biscuits her full-time job (she wouldn't recommend it as a career to others), she loves baking for dogs as a hobby and a way to help animal welfare groups at events.

"Sometimes I miss being a doctor," Geri says. "But I love being a baker and a businesswoman. I wish I could have done all three."

Unusual Eating Habits

Not all dogs approach mealtime in the same way. Some dogs hoover their food. Others graze daintily over time like cats.

When Rufus was a puppy, he was fed in the vicinity of two older dogs, who tried to get his food when they finished theirs. His guardian, Peggy Sherman, thought they would work it out, as had many previous dogs. "This was a huge mistake on our part," Peggy says. "Rufus never got over it and it seriously affected his attitude toward food and eating in general."

If you have several dogs, try feeding them in separate pens or rooms so the slow eaters can take their sweet time.

He eats alone and undisturbed now, and has for more than three years, but it has made no difference in his attitude. "If he catches sight of one of us through the doorway, he will begin what sounds like ferocious snarling and will actually lunge at the door," she says. She did, however, figure out that his behavior is related to eating dog food from a bowl or plate. So she started making "Rufus cookies" for supper. These are large baked cookies made with whole wheat flour, peanut butter, eggs, powdered milk, water, and garlic powder, or a separate recipe using low-salt chicken broth instead of peanut butter. "He will take pieces out of our hand and does not care if we arrange pieces in front of him (not on a plate or bowl) right under his nose," Peggy says. "His behavior is completely different with the cookies."

Chance, Claudine Randazzo's German shorthaired pointer, developed a habit of refusing to eat unless Claudine hugged and kissed her at mealtime. She would stand and stare at her bowl waiting for a love-up. After about a month of this, Claudine's husband started spooning a few tablespoons of elk-meat stew on Chance's kibble. "Ever since we started doing that," Claudine says, "she has forgotten completely about the hugging and kissing." OK, so this isn't a tip. But it is a cute story and elk stew sounds like something any dog would love.

Mix it up.

Throw kibble (the smaller the better) out into the backyard and let your dog scavenge for it. Arna Dan Isacsson, who lives with a score of rehabilitated sled dogs in Fairbanks, Alaska, calls this "broadcast feeding" or "adventure feeding." It's a little like wild foraging and adds variety to mealtime. She also varies the food experience with raw and cooked meals, frozen meat, fish, and fast days. Some days, the dogs get to clean up after she chops meat; other days, they feast on raw bones, raw whole turkey necks, and raw chicken thigh bones. "I also have a 'Bone Yard,' where I bury day-old bones," she says. "They love to dig them up and re-bury them and strut around."

Pet-proof the kitchen.

Dani Baker's four dachshunds are serious chowhounds, who regularly raided the kitchen. At one point two of them, Howie and Molly, ingested a bag of chocolate chips and pancake mix (and survived!). But Molly was the chronic offender, often looking like a miniature potbellied pig for a few days after a plunder. So Dani did what any self-respecting parent would do: She secured the kitchen cabinets in her Seattle home with childproof locks.

Place an enterprising, gourmet dog in the home of a chef-caterer and snack happens. While Christie Withers was living

and cooking in the Bay Area, her poodle Wizard learned to nudge open her conventional-design refrigerator. He only took meat and cheese, and he rarely left a mess. The real problem was that he didn't learn how to close the fridge, so the rest of the food spoiled. At a friend's recommendation, Christie tried sealing the door with strips of Velcro. This baffled Wizard for only a few days—then he was back eating Camembert and beef tenderloin. The fix? She screwed an eyebolt into her wall and wrapped a bungee cord around the refrigerator handle and through the eyebolt. Wizard never cracked that safe. Because Christie continues to live with poodles, all her future refrigerators have been of a nudge-proof design.

When securing the kitchen, don't forget the dishwasher. Remember Chester? I mentioned him earlier. He's the wee troublemaker my cousins adopted. During a dinner party clean-up session, he decided to help with dish duty by prelicking the plates in the dishwasher. When he was discovered, he beat a hasty retreat, except he was so deep in dishware at the time, his collar hooked on something and he took the entire rack with him—smashing a full serving of plates to smithereens.

At Home

HOME IS WHERE THE POOCH IS—and also the fur-bunnies and the drool and the paw prints and the chewed chair legs and the shredded squeaky toys. Some days sharing our homes with dogs feels like hosting a pack of muddy hyenas for lunch. While puppies have their own more-demanding homecare requirements, living with a *trained* adult dog (notice the emphasis on trained) doesn't have to mean a life of constant vigilance, grimy couches, and dander odor. Even the doyenne of gracious living, Martha Stewart, keeps house with chows chows and French bulldogs—albeit with a small army of helpers. Fastidious folks with dog-loving genes have engineered all sorts of methods for keeping an elegant and clean home, methods they are happy to share.

DOG-SMART HOME DESIGN

We begin with the bones—if you'll forgive the pun —a look at dog-smart design strategies that don't require turning your house into a labyrinth of child gates or making your dog feel miserable and left out. The central goal here is to set up your domicile so that you and your dog enjoy the cozy indoors.

Sometimes you get lucky. Sally Oien, an interior designer in Seattle, lives with Gus, an "underdog." Gus's favorite spot in the house is under the dining room table with a long view of the living room. If Gus were a Great Dane, entry and exit could pose some problems. But she's a compact Border collie mix, and her self-selected den is a perfect, out-of-the-way place for her to chill. When Claudine Randazzo, a writer in Flagstaff, Arizona, rescued a rottweiler–Doberman mix named Bo, he commandeered an unused fireplace for the first few months in his new home. (More about him in a minute.)

Sally's advice is to respond to your dog's natural inclinations and use furniture arrangement to channel them; that is, create comfortable, inviting spaces where you want dogs to hang out and make no-go zones less hospitable.

Priority One: A Perch

Most dogs will seek out a window view—for sunbathing or squirrel watching. If you're smart it will be in a spot you designate. Lulu lies for a good part of the day in front of our glass front door waiting for the UPS dude, Jehovah's Witnesses, and BoBo, a notoriously confrontational neighborhood cat. We selected the door to bring light into our living room. But it has become so much more.

For other dogs, it's the back of the couch, a window seat, or a bench. If you decide on the spot and make it comfortable, you can control where your dog hangs out. This is a positive avenue for keeping your dog off some furniture.

When Claudine and her husband remodeled their home in Flagstaff, they selected glass French doors to give their dogs, Bo and Chance, easy access to the view of the 13,000-foot San Francisco peaks. "They just live for that," she says.

For Bo, big views are especially important. Claudine rescued him after two years in a junkyard and three more kicking around shelters and foster care. They took him camping the very first week they were together. As far as Claudine knows, he'd never been in the wilderness. At one point in camp, they lost track of him. "When we looked behind the tent, he was sitting up on this ridge, staring out on this whole mountain range," Claudine says. "It was like he was taking it all in. I just cried." These days Bo can spend hours appreciating the mountain view.

Pet-Friendly Furniture

"We try to get furniture so we don't have to kick the dogs off," Claudine says. "We subscribe to the idea that pack animals are happiest with their pack." She opted for a rustic leather couch, so she can just wipe the fur off.

Similarly, Cindy Trimble Kelly, an interior designer in Blue Ridge, Georgia, doesn't see the reason for keeping dogs off all the furniture (or outside, for that matter). Cuddling with her three corgis is an important daily ritual. She works hard to encourage people with pets to create pet-friendly environments. When one client planned to upgrade her cabin and institute a new regime relegating her two middle-aged Great Danes elsewhere for the first time, Cindy protested. Instead of thoroughly hurting the dogs' feelings and missing out on couch-time together, she suggested washable slipcovers over nice upholstery (which could be revealed for guests). The best of both worlds.

Another simpler option is a special blanket or throw for chairs or couches. This requires some training—rewarding your pooch when she curls up to sleep on the blanket, rather than directly on the couch. Select washable throws. Susan Hilger, an interior designer in Charlotte, North Carolina, backs her cotton throws with flannel or bamboo fabric so they don't slip and slide. (A plus for bamboo, she says, is its antimicrobial qualities.) Having different fabric on each side helps you to keep track of the furry, "dog" side. Old sheets and towels work in a pinch as well.

Some fabrics are more dog-resistant than others. Ultrasuede and distressed leather hold up well, as does Crypton Super Fabric, which has a moisture barrier that is odor- and stain-resistant. For upholstery or carpet, select materials with texture, patterns, and multiple colors. A solid color will always show soil more quickly.

Susan Hilger's trick for removing animal hair from furniture: Wear rubber gloves. Fur sticks to them.

Why not buy dogs their own furniture? There are now such fancy couches and loungers for dogs, they might have to kick you off.

Maintain no-go zones.
There's obviously nothing wrong with training your dogs to stay off the couch. In fact, many trainers recommend human furniture and beds be off limits as a way to maintain a certain level of leadership. To maintain rule of law while you're away, lay tin foil across sofa cushions. The crinkle noise is a great deterrent. My sister Eileen Wogan does this to keep her two cats off the bed and discovered it works for many dogs as well. I also knew a couple who put transmitters for an electronic containment system, like an Invisible Fence, under sofas and easy chairs to keep the dogs off.

The Lowdown on Keeping Life Low Down
Many dogs leap on and off furniture dozens of times a day. If you have stairs in your home, that's more Olympic hurdling. Over the course of a decade, all this impact adds up to injuries including, but certainly not limited to, broken toenails, sprains, dislocations, and tissue degeneration. This is especially tough on dogs with small legs and long bodies, such as dachshunds.

Money saver: If you need to use a baby gate to block off stairs, find a used freebie through the Freecycle Network (find your local Freecycle community at *www.freecycle.org*).

The key is to eliminate jumping, with low furniture, ramps, intermediate stairs, and training. Ramps are especially good for dogs with arthritis. This isn't just a small-breed issue. Larger dogs don't need the wear and tear on knees and hips. Sally Oien was glad her bed was low to the ground after Gus's ACL surgery. Don't forget ramps for outdoor stairs.

After pricing pet stairs, elementary school teacher Briana Solovitz fabricated a step next to her bed for her pug, Miguel Raoul. She glued a carpet remnant to a milk crate. It's the perfect intermediate height.

A bonus for blind dogs: Carpeted ramps can also be an asset for visually-impaired pups in a home with stairs. One family used strips of indoor-outdoor carpet to map a dog route through the house, onto the porch, and down a ramp into the backyard. Nicole Gendics in Cleveland puts various scented oils on her door frames so her blind dog knows which room she is entering.

When my husband and I retired our sleigh bed for something closer to the floor for our bed-loving Lulu, we upgraded to a king-size mattress. It worked for our friends with young children, and it works for us.

While we're on the subject, remember not everyone loves "pack bed" to the same degree. "My boyfriend got sick of filthy sheets on the bed," says Seattle author Michelle Goodman, who admits she was often a little lazy about changing them. "So we enacted a new policy: We use a cover sheet and always make the bed. Less sheet washing, more snuggling with Buddy!" Flannel works well, especially for dogs with oily fur, like Labs, because the fur sticks to the flannel instead of drifting all over.

Floors Are for Spooning

Our standards for floors are different than our dogs'. Why wouldn't they be? Canines enjoy a much more intimate relationship (sometimes mere centimeters) with the terrain beneath our feet. We walk the floor—often wearing shoes. They sit on it. Sleep on it. Roll on it. Eat off it. So folks who think about these things say to pick durable, natural products for floors that are easy on dogs and also good looking and easy to maintain for you.

Dog-loving interior designer Susan Hilger prefers hard-surface floors, specifically tile, laminates, and bamboo (which are eco-friendly)—durable and easy to clean. She also likes dyed concrete, using nontoxic, water-based pigments. With bamboo, she suggests not staining it, since it can be scratched. Laminates are durable, easy to clean, and easy on the budget.

Like many dog folk, she stays away from carpet, but for clients who insist on something wall-to-wall she recommends modular carpet tiles. If a pet stains one of the tiles, it can be pulled up, cleaned, and put back down or replaced. For example, FLOR-brand carpet tiles (some of which are even named after animals) have antimicrobial agents that inhibit molds and bacteria.

Think about flooring in terms of how you and your dogs will use the house. Susan used slate in her home entryway, which takes the brunt of dog dirt. Tile is great for entry rooms, grooming areas, and mudrooms.

Warm up cold floors.

"If you can put in radiant floors, it is the dog's favorite thing in the world," Sally Oien says. "I've seen them sprawled out on warm concrete." This is most practical in a new or extensively remodeled house. Of course, some dogs, especially northern breeds, dogs with dense fur, or dogs in warm climates love to chill on cool tile. Variety is the spice of life.

Deploy area rugs.

Bolster your border patrol with washable, dirt-trapping doormats in front of doors. They attract and hold dust particles. Small area rugs can make for cushy snooze spots on otherwise easy-to-clean surfaces, but don't forget no-slip rug pads to keep zany puppies from taking magic carpet rides.

Choose hardwood.

Avoid maple and cherry, which are soft and can be damaged by dog claws, particularly with big dogs. Opt for hickory, oak, and heart pine in these cases. Thin laminate wood floors are also easily damaged by claws.

In the case of bamboo and wood, be sure floors are sealed against water bowl splashes, soggy paws, or wet bellies. A plastic or otherwise water-resistant placemat under a water bowl can help manage drips.

Try vinyls and other alternatives.
When Nicole Gendics rescued a dog who suffered from a serious kidney condition for several months, she realized the carpet in her Cleveland home would have to go. Rather than fret herself sick and upset the dog, she pulled up the carpet and replaced it with vinyl.

One thing to watch out for with vinyl: It's inexpensive and easy to clean, but in some cases it releases harmful gases for many years. Do you want your beloved pal sleeping on that? There are lots of natural alternatives such as linoleum and Marmoleum.

Going with natural, eco-friendly floors for the dogs who sleep, eat, and play on them is good for us and for the environment.

Dog Room

A dog room can be everything from a space for feeding and storage to an actual bedroom. In Claudine Randazzo's former home in California, a rarely used kitchen nook became an out-of-the-way dog space for elevated food and water bowls and food storage.

Another option is a mudroom near an entrance. Folks suggest amenities such as a walk-in shower with a handheld sprayer for rinsing puppy paws, and a dog door to the backyard. It's great if the mudroom is in or near the laundry room.

Remember wet, dirty dogs love to shake off or rub up against walls, leaving oils and a dingy cast. Susan Hilger recommends low- to no-VOC eggshell or satin paints. (VOC—volatile organic compounds—are highly evaporative chemicals found in paints, stains, and similar products that can cause breathing problems, rashes, and other health concerns.) These are easier to clean than flat paints and easier on the environment you and your dogs share.

Cat House?

When cats and dogs live under the same roof, it can be equally important to carve out a dog-free niche for cats—especially if your dog likes kitty chow or raiding the litter box. Interior designer Cindy Trimble Kelly partnered with one of her clients to transform a closet into a "cat house." It was accessed by a small cat door, through which the dog couldn't fit. Inside the closet was a motion detector, which heated the room and illuminated the cat's food, water, and a litter box every time she entered. This closet had another ingenious detail: a back door that opened into the garage, so that the cat's owner could clean the litter box in the garage and never bring it into the house.

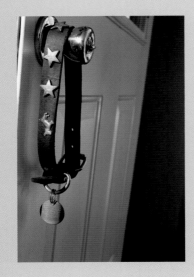

Designer Elements

Even though we share our homes with dogs, that's no excuse to let style go *to the dogs*. Here are a few ways dogs' house-mates let function inspire form.

- *Raised dog bowls:* Dog bowl stands can be expensive, clunky, and downright ugly. Dog photographer Bev Sparks learned from a friend about using wrought-iron plant stands as a cheaper, slimmer, funkier alternative.
- *Outdoor toy box:* A ceramic plant container—with a drain hole—can be a fitting toy holder for a patio.
- *Poop bag stations:* When Sally Oien's neighbor collects her morning newspaper, she slips off the one or two protective plastic bags—perfect for poop collection—and pops them in an outdoor box before she goes inside. Sally suggests using an old mailbox and turning it into an interesting visual element. "I always forget bags," she says. "So I have to go back in and turn the alarm off. In this case, they're right outside, where they should be."

Thanks to recycling buffs, fabric sleeves for storing plastic bags indoors are pretty inexpensive and sold in tree-hugger catalogs and stores. My sister Whitney sewed her own—and says it's a snap. For a more industrial, less portable dispenser, bolt a foot-and-a-half long PVC pipe to the wall, and stuff the bags in there.

Dog Beds

The good news with beds—which are about the boldest "dog statement" many folks will have in their home—is that they are better engineered, better looking, and greener than ever before.

Turn cleanup into a game or training opportunity by teaching your dogs to put their toys away. Arna Dan Isacsson lives with twenty-plus dogs in Fairbanks and expects them to put indoor toys in the indoor box and leave outdoor toys outdoors.

Shop around to find the right bed for you and your dog—your choices are nearly unlimited. From faux sheepskin and corduroy to leopard and zebra prints, beds come in every shape and size, with head rests, orthopedic detailing, cooling elements, and personalization. Among the many brands are old catalog faithfuls like L.L. Bean and Doctors Foster and Smith, and high-end lines such as Bowsers, Bella Dogga (made from organic cotton denim), and Haute Pooch (which makes a bed with a hood for teacup-size buddies). My dog, Lulu, loves her Big Shrimpy bed, stuffed with fleece pieces, recycled off the cutting room floor of clothing manufacturers. The entire bed, stuffing included, is easily machine washable.

Get-well bed: Seattleite Lynn T. needed a special bed for her dog, Nell, a Newfoundland with paralyzed back legs. Nell spent long hours on her store-bought pad and developed a dangerous bedsore. Inspired by an ad for buckwheat hull pillows (which claimed the pillows would draw away heat and moisture), Lynn purchased two twenty-pound bags of buckwheat hull seeds and her sister sewed them into a bed, which Nell slept on without any further bedsores.

DOGS AT THE OFFICE

If you work at home with your dog or bring him to the office, post signs. Cindy brings her three corgis—Peanut, Bandita, and Lucy—to work, where they are joined by three other corgis who live with her office manager. In the front yard Cindy posted a little "Corgi Country" flag with an image of the big-eared dog in a cowboy hat. In addition, there are signs on all the doors warning that dogs are inside and doors should be closed after entering or exiting. This helps protect against bolters and also gives fair warning to newcomers who may not be all that comfortable around dogs.

Conceal cables.

Cables look like toys to puppies and chew hounds. Conceal electrical wires with store-bought cord organizers or under a milk crate.

Extract fur from the keyboard.

"Tired of paying five dollars a can for air to clean your computer keyboard?" asks Suzie deDisse, a volunteer with the Evergreen Animal Protection League in Colorado. She suggests a silicone pastry brush to pull pet hair and other debris off your keyboard with a couple of sweeps along the keys.

Set a policy.

If you have more than one or two people in the office, you may have to establish a pet policy. At the Mountaineers Books, my publisher, employees can bring dogs to work one day a week. And there are rules: Any dog who barks at visitors is sent home, and no dogs are allowed in the lunch or conference rooms. In addition, a neutral person (a.k.a. non-dog owner) is designated as the go-to guy for anyone to discuss issues about the dog policy.

FIGHTING STAINS, FUR BALLS, AND DOG-ROMA

My sister Whitney, her daughters, Olivia and Hailey, and her husband, Matt, are top-flight dog people in every way. They recently rescued two young dogs—Zipper and Zooma. They spend hours training, playing, walking, visiting the off-leash park, and snuggling. But after years with a well-trained, geriatric Lab, who died a few years ago, they weren't prepared for the domestic impact of two puppies. The off-white carpet in their Boulder home is now off-off-off white and smells a little of eau du chien and stain remover. Their plush, ivory couch looks like a science project. When I asked my normally fastidious sister for her housekeeping advice for the book, she was succinct: "Lower your standards."

While my description of her living room may not inspire you (or please her), Whitney's attitude certainly makes everyone she lives with—pups included—a lot happier. Here's my key takeaway from the housekeeping trenches: You are living with furry, independent creatures. Don't make yourself crazy pretending otherwise. If you live with animals, it can be a good idea to believe that no object is all that important.

Do the Roomba!

Everyone has their long-standing vacuum loyalties—Dyson, Rainbow, Miele, among them—but the Roomba (made by iRobot) adds excitement to the whole dog-fur battle. The disc-shaped, battery-operated robotic pod (which looks like a flying saucer) makes its own random way around a room, following a wall here and ricocheting off a couch there, eventually sucking up lots of dirt and fur, while you're out playing with your dog. Roombas are not perfect—for example, they have to be emptied frequently—but the dog folks I've talked to say they provide a helpful bulwark against furry tumbleweeds.

Urine Town

Urine, especially in old carpets or comforters, has a way of hiding. I know a trainer who encouraged people not to sleep with their dogs—at least not while they were young puppies or if they were misbehaving. (The puppies, that is.) For those who didn't want to banish small dogs with even smaller bladders from the bedroom, the trainer resorted to a little visual exposé. She'd shine a handheld black light in a darkened bedroom, revealing urine stains past and present. The results were often très Jackson Pollock. After the shock wore off, the somewhat chastened dog cuddlers could use the decoder light to attack old and new urine stains, or to convince themselves to get rid of the sheets, mattress, carpet . . . the entire house.

Even after you scrub a urine spot, while you can't see it or smell it, dogs still can. Unless you use a cleanser with an enzymatic element, your dog will return to the spot to cover it, even those who have been house-trained. Don't set your dog up for that sort of failure.

Mama Aud's stain fighter: My mother-in-law, Audrey Fischer, is not a faint-hearted housekeeper. She has lived with dogs and white carpets for decades in the often muddy, wet climes of Duluth, Minnesota. Although her last buddy, a toy poodle named Ernie, died a couple years ago, she still finds opportunities to employ the old dog-stain removal method when her grandchildren visit. Here it is:

First, saturate the stain with club soda. Next, take a bath towel and blot up the liquid. This can take some time, lots of stepping on the towel and finding new dry spots and stepping again. Once you've absorbed as much club soda as you can, dust the stain liberally with cornstarch. Let it dry. Not for an hour. Not for a few hours. Sometimes for as long as a couple days. The cornstarch will absorb the color of the stain. When it's dry, vacuum up the cornstarch and cleanup accomplished!

Housekeeping humans can be fiercely loyal to stain fighters that work. Favorite store-bought solutions include: Nature's Miracle (also known as Petastic, which one intrepid dog lover discovered also works well on red wine stains), Get Serious, Resolve, See Spot Go, Simple Solution, Anti-Icky-Poo, PetZyme, Spot Shot, Urine-Off, Urine Gone.

For some additional freshening while you power sweep, try dropping an unused, spicy herbal tea bag into the vacuum bag before you start. The scent helps mask fur odor. The stronger the spice blend—clove, nutmeg, cinnamon, chai, anise—the better it works.

Learn to love vinegar.

When a dog is your roommate, vinegar is your best friend. White vinegar is the stuff for all natural, dog-friendly cleaning. If you've got an unrepentant toilet-water guzzler, vinegar is a nice alternative to bleach. Clean the bowl by adding a cup, closing the lid, and leaving it overnight. Remove nose prints on glass—remember this for the car—with a vinegar and water spray. Old-fashioned types wipe with newspaper. Vinegar also eliminates drool-sheen in a dog bowl. Add a half-cup of vinegar to a gallon of water for a dog-safe floor wash, and splash it in the rinse cycle when washing pee-stained towels, sheets, or throw rugs.

Mary "Mimi" Hill of Durant, Oklahoma, suggests mixing a cup of vinegar in any sudsy solution of your own choosing for spots. She also adds a cup to Bissell's Pet Odor and Stain removal formula when she steam-cleans carpets.

Mimi learned about vinegar in nursing school, when she did a term paper in chemistry on yeast/fungal inhibitors. But the real source of her knowledge was her mother, who told her it was the DOC (douche-of-choice) during WWII. She uses plain white distilled vinegar and cotton for cleaning out dog ears. Rinsing a dog with vinegar is also said to act as a flea repellent and to help with hot spots.

Turn home-smelly-home back into home-sweet-home.

- Clean frequently. Use green cleaners that won't harm your pet. Remember dogs like to lick surfaces.
- Seek out products that are designed to neutralize odors.
- Interior designer Cindy Trimble Kelly washes her corgis frequently to keep her home and office from smelling like canines, which would be a real turnoff for her clients. She also cleans her work and living spaces frequently and lights scented candles. (For a retirement community she worked on, she insisted the developer include a dog-wash station in the clubhouse.)
- Susan Hilger changes the filters on her furnace regularly and buys more expensive filters that catch pet dander and hair as well as other allergens in the air.

GREEN PAWS

Usually when people talk about dogs in the garden, it's with derision or lament. Our furry friends, the complaints go, leave brown spots in the lawn, dig holes, and pluck plump tomatoes off the vine. But there is a new generation of dog-loving gardeners and pragmatic landscape architects learning to embrace the challenge, seeking more than mere coexistence. They aim to create lush environments that fulfill the deeper urges of green thumbs and bone-munchers alike.

The central idea is to let your dog drive some of your gardening choices. Dogs love to run through the branches of weeping trees and tall grasses, climb rocks or knolls, sleep in the shade of a tree, or slurp from a water feature. The byword with dog-friendly gardens is to work with, and not against, your dog's instincts.

Create splish-splash stations.

Of course the ultimate for many dogs is a pond (or even a fountain). Water can provide a bowl, a place to cool off, and a bird bath—all of which keep dogs entertained. Lisa Port, a landscape designer and owner of Banyon Tree Design Studio in Seattle, has designed several gardens with dogs in mind. For Copper and Shiner, two English setters, she created a boulder-lined waterfall and pond. (There is also a flagstone area with an outdoor spigot, where the dogs can be rinsed off.)

The boundary between this backyard and the neighbor's house is open, creating more space for Copper and Shiner, and also for Agnes, the black Lab who used to live next door. She liked to amble over and take a cooling wade in the setters' pond. Her family has since moved, but she has a pond and waterfall at her new home.

Briana Solovitz likes to sit in the sun on her back deck in O'Fallon, Missouri, during summer break. For her dog, Miguel, she created a "Puggy Oasis," a blue plastic wading pool (and drinking tub) with rubber ducks and a lounging mat, all in the shade of an umbrella.

There is a pragmatic reason for adding play elements in your garden for your dog's entertainment. "Dogs can get bored in their spaces. If you make them happy, you will protect the garden," says Robin Haglund, a landscape designer and owner of Garden Mentors in Seattle. She has worked with and around her own and clients' dogs for years.

Give them a place to dig.

It can be tough to break the habits of a born digger, such as a terrier. Instead, consider a digging pit. "Create a sandbox for your dog," Robin suggests. "Then bury toys with treats in them to train a dog to dig in that particular spot." She also encourages gardeners to avoid digging in front of their dogs. "Some may learn from seeing your work and try to mimic it," she explains.

A kiddie pool is an inexpensive and portable option for a digging pit. Old tin tubs, troughs, or wood barrels, which are often sold as planters, are other options.

Train them.

This brings us to an important aspect of dog-friendly gardens: Smart design is just a start. Most gardeners have to train their dogs to share the garden.

An open plan invites failure. Dog-friendly gardeners deploy barriers, arbors, decorative stakes, and pathways to funnel dogs' energies away from perishables. With his older dogs, Jenny and Cleo, Matt Cohn used temporary two-foot fencing around flowers and vegetables in his Boulder garden, which they were trained to respect. For his young dogs, Hazel and Rosie, these fragile cues aren't enough yet.

In places where dogs are welcome, landscape designer Lisa Port selects pet-friendly plants, such as soft evergreens, and eschews pokey plants or plants with burrs or sticky seedpods. While we're on the subject of plant selection, there are many plants that are toxic for dogs. (As with foods, the ASPCA posts on its website a list of plants that can harm animals, *www.aspca.org.*)

Raise beds.

In one gated backyard, Lisa Port created twenty-four-inch raised fruit-and-vegetable beds. Wide grassy spaces in between act as an informal dog run for a pair of English setters. The dogs stay out of the edibles and, as a surprise bonus, their presence keeps birds out of the strawberries. "I am no expert," she says. "I'm really just taking cues from the dog owners themselves. And there have been some unexpected benefits that everyone is enjoying."

Mend fences.

Lisa is currently designing a yard that will be home to a small dog. She's taking the obvious step of making sure the fence is set in the ground so the pup can't slip under. But she and her clients are also considering adding windows in the fence, so he can see out.

Avoid chicken wire or other wires underground where dogs stage their great escapes. "Wires may keep them from digging, but paw and claw damage can be extensive," Robin Haglund says. "If your dog escapes by digging below fence lines, dig a trench yourself and fill it with gravel and pavers." These will discourage everyone except your Steve McQueen–inspired dogs.

Don't wait to dog-proof your yard (or your house for that matter) until after your dog has arrived. When Wendy Hughes-Jelen first brought Sophia, an Italian greyhound, to her Seattle home, the yard wasn't fully fenced. It took two rain-soaked months to complete. "These dogs hate rain, and her bladder is the size of a walnut," Wendy says. "I'd be out at three o' clock in the morning in my bathrobe and tennis shoes, saying, 'Go potty. Go potty.'"

Ever notice how the dirt dug out of a hole is never enough to fill the hole again? And how once a hole is dug, it is inexorably redug time and time again? At the Marymoor Park off-leash area in Redmond, Washington, Judy Trockel has figured out how to keep dogs from redigging old holes. She fills them with gravel, the only effective fix she's found.

If you've got a mulch-eater, you'll want to test a small sample area before spreading it all over your garden, Robin Haglund says. Cocoa mulches, in particular, can be toxic to dogs.

Check out zoning laws. Some homeowners discovered too late that their planned development wouldn't allow them to fence their backyard.

Urine Town, Redux

Brown spots in the lawn: the true dogs-in-the-yard Waterloo, as well as a wellspring of misinformation. One of the common things you hear around the plastic bag dispenser is that pH in dog urine is the problem, and that feeding your dog tomato juice or chlorophyll bones will fix it. But it looks like the high concentration of nitrogen is the culprit, "burning" grass and other plants. So there's no true dietary solution.

Some dog-friendly gardeners create "break" areas out of stone, gravel, or sweet-smelling cedar chips and train dogs to relieve themselves there. For a particularly shy pooch, Robin Haglund even created a gravel pad with a plant screen for privacy. Now that's dog friendly!

Another option is a sort of canine Honey Bucket. In anticipation of a move from a house with a large yard to a condo with a balcony, Wendy Hughes-Jelen purchased a product called a Pet Loo for her Italian greyhound. The Pet Loo consists of a black plastic square covered in synthetic, odor-eating grass. Looking a bit like a small putting green, it provides that median of grass for your pet anywhere you need it—a mudroom, a balcony, even in the backyard. The urine is collected in a drawer for disposal and the entire thing can be easily dismantled and washed down.

Flea-control tip: Sometimes a little grassroots dog wisdom finds its way into the *New York Times*. A story about dogs in Appalachia included a folk remedy for controlling fleas and ticks. Tobacco chewers save the juice and spray it on the lawn.

Honorable mention: Newspaper bag. Is there anything more perfectly designed for a job it was not designed to do?

Enter the poop-patrol sweepstakes.

It seems nothing inspires innovation like dog waste. Or, to be more precise, dog waste removal. It's a stinky, messy job that gets the creative juices flowing. Ingenuity is the hallmark of the three grassroots pooper scoopers described below.

After a neighbor injured his back picking up dog waste, Randy Waltz got busy with a solution. His Blue Ribbon Scooper is a long-handled grabber, equipped with two stainless steel claws (rounded teeth that fit together). A trigger at the handle end opens and closes the claws. The long handle lets you pick up dog waste without bending over, and then tilt the filled scooper at an angle to drop the waste into a plastic bag attached to the claws. A former software writer, Waltz continues to be motivated by dog-doo. He is currently developing a scooper caddy and cleaner.

Minnesotan Martin Dehen patented a small, plastic scoop that slips onto the blade of a hockey stick, transforming it into a mighty poop-flinger. For novice hockey players, the Turd Burglar comes with a free rubber practice poop. All you need is a hockey stick, a compost pile or collection bin, and a sense of humor.

Poop Freeze is a chlorofluorocarbon-free aerosol spray that when misted onto a waste pile forms a frozen shell for a couple minutes—long enough for smudge-free pickup. "Just frost and toss!" says Aaron Udler, the dog-loving pitchman behind this space-age solution. Invented a few years ago by a "mad scientist" friend of his in Rockville, Maryland, Poop Freeze has made believers out of dog walkers with many charges and solo nonprofessionals. Most people, Aaron says, want a can in reserve for the rare but especially swashy cases.

BAD FUR DAYS

Every dog has them. Caked with mud or marinated in an unidentifiable stink from the park, dogs can't always wait for a professional to tackle their grooming challenges. At some point, all of us will undertake the groomer's art, whether it's waging the battle of the suds, sweetening up a pooch's dragon breath, or performing pedicures on tender paws.

Bev Sparks gives her dogless Seattle neighbors biscuits to occasionally pitch over the fence to her dogs on the assumption this will help her neighbors know and like the dogs and tolerate the occasional bark alert. It's also helped build connection where one often finds friction.

SECOND ACT: FROM TENDING BAR TO TIDYING TURF

Ten years ago, George Gadda was inspired by Pacino to start a business (not Pacino the actor, Pacino the dog—George's Akita). Like so many entrepreneurs in the new dog economy, George saw an opportunity to be his own boss and leave the world of tending bar. But he didn't follow a road more traveled. Instead, the veteran bartender did what bartenders do best—he listened. He asked people what they liked and didn't like about having a dog. He learned that a universal downside to life with a dog was cleaning up after them.

Eureka! With a partner, George started Tidy Turf, a pet-waste removal service. In private backyards, rescue shelters, dog parks, and anywhere else dogs like to do their business in California's Marin and Sonoma counties, George follows soon after with a plastic-lined bucket, scooper, and rubber gloves. It's a straightforward, surprisingly clean job, except when muddy dogs jump on him.

Slippery When Wet

When it comes to giving our canine friends their baths, the X-factor is, of course, the groomee. Who was it who said you can lead a dog to water but you can't make him bathe? She was *so* right. At the sight of no-tears shampoo, bath-hating dogs are transformed from cuddly bunnies to Beelzebub. They snarl. They scratch. They scream. They nip. Or, they just stand still, so mournful and dejected it breaks your heart.

Even devoted swimmers tremble and scurry under patio furniture at the first uncurling of a hose. (Maybe the only thing more dreaded is nail trimming. More on that later.) We'll leave the psychology of this liquid love-hate for greater minds to plumb and focus on time-tested solutions from the bathrooms and backyards of North America.

Deploy sponges for the waterphobic.

We begin with the bath because that, Virginia, is where sweet-smelling, shiny dogs are born. But when water is the problem, what's to be done? Caitlin in Kitchener, Ontario, has

For some dogs, the sound of water spraying from a showerhead is the deal breaker. Try using a flexible shower hose without the spray head.

From the It-Should-Be-Obvious-But-Bears-Repeating files: Home groomers should make sure their dogs take a pee break before the bath, so they don't have to run outdoors while wet. That's a hard-won lesson from Renee Hensley. She lives with Onyx, a German shepherd, in North Pole, Alaska, where winter temperatures often drop to forty below.

developed a "water-lite" approach for washing Bailey, her H_2O-averse pug–Chihuahua mix. She forged her strategy in that crucible of grooming—washing a cat.

Caitlin avoids the big water effect of a full tub or the spray sound of a showerhead. Instead, she fills four buckets with warm water. One is for shampoo; the other three are for rinsing. She keeps about six sponges on hand, three with conditioner pre-squeezed on them. Beginning in a dry bathtub, she sponges soapy water on Bailey. Then she lathers, rinses, and repeats, if necessary. Then she rinses again and applies conditioner, leaving it on for five minutes. She rinses again, thoroughly. When she thinks she'd rather die than rinse some more, she rinses one last time.

Caitlin rewards Bailey with a long, drying snuggle in a warm towel, which he loves. The sponge-and-bucket technique works so well, Caitlin washes Bailey and her Himalayan Siamese cat, Muffin, at the same time, which sort of seems like pushing the envelope. But apparently it works.

Time-saver tip: For time-strapped multitaskers, there's always showering together. Mali McGolden in Seattle trained her piebald dachshund, Dash, to follow her into the tile rainforest. While her other three dachshunds get the utility sink treatment, this sturdy pup with a Lab self-image trots blithely into the shower. Now, if she could only get her to dry herself off. I've heard of other dogs showering with their guardians—just keep in mind that too much of a good thing can dry out some dogs' coats.

BUDGET BUSTER

Fashionable-types on a budget have long known that beauty schools can be an inexpensive alternative for cutting-edge hair care. So why not have your dog groomed at a reputable grooming school? John and Kyle Hoving share their one-bedroom apartment on Manhattan's Upper East Side with three ottoman-size golden retrievers and a nineteen-year-old cat. Keeping Tyson, Tracey, and Keeper looking as elegant as their zip code can run more than one hundred dollars per dog at a neighborhood groomer. So John takes his posse downtown to the New York School of Dog Grooming for a shampoo, brush, blow dry, and nail trimming at one-third the price of a regular groomer. There are grooming schools in most cities; see if one near you needs dog models.

Ward off the chill.

Not all dogs can be washed in tubs or even in bathrooms. Many big breeds must suffer the chill of hose water along with the trauma of bathing. Before Doina Berndt washed Thor, her Newfoundland–Great Dane mix, she would connect six hoses together, fill them with water, and let them heat in the sun of her Oklahoma City backyard. Voila, a warm rinse. A kiddie pool warmed in the sun simulates a "hot" tub experience.

Dress for soapy success.

- *Wear a swimsuit or an old T-shirt and shorts.* Your wardrobe for bathing your dog should consist only of clothes that can get soaking wet and covered in fur, dirt, even blood. Intrepid home groomers say joining your dog in the bath, with lots of belly rubs and massage, helps make it a more positive experience. Don't let sartorial worries increase your difficulty factor.
- *Use eye protection.* Dogs love a soggy, soapy shake. If you are worried about soap in your eyes or contacts, wear glasses, sunglasses, or even goggles.
- *Include a waterproof treat pouch.* Keep essential rewards easy to reach and dry with a pouch at your waist.

Hang on Snoopy.

Like driving with a cell phone, it's hard to wash a dog and hold onto a collar or leash at the same time. Some folks recommend tying off your dog's leash with a quick-release knot to a soap dish or a bench. If your pup's in the tub, you want the lead long enough so he can maneuver but not jump out. Outside, you want room to move, but not enough tether to trip you up. Many dogs will learn, and accept, the limits of the restraint. More importantly, it frees up your hands to get the job done more quickly, which is better for everyone. Remember: Never leave your dog in the tub on the tether alone.

If you wash your dog in the tub, be sure to place a rubber bath mat on the bottom so your dog's feet don't slip around, which can be unsettling.

Tucker Madsen, a miniature schnauzer in Orlando, Florida, gets an almost empty can of peanut butter at grooming time. When he's neck deep in all that oily goodness, he forgets his passionate hatred for bath time. Other people spread a little PB directly on the tub rim.

Even if your dog is fairly manageable, she is slippery when wet, so close the door to the bathing room or use a leash to avoid a soppy juggernaut leaping onto the couch.

Keep inner ears dry.

A dog's head is an extremely kissable quadrant, but it's also home to the muzzle, a mechanism for probing the stinky universe at our feet. It must be washed—if gingerly. Lots of lay groomers use no-tears shampoo for children on their pet's face, and there are dog formulations as well. Another concern when washing a dog's head is getting water in the ears. Try gently tucking cotton balls in the ear openings to avoid that problem. Apparently, it's an old groomer's trick.

Trash someone else's tub.

When it's time to wash her big dogs (a pair of Great Pyrenees, each averaging more than a hundred furry pounds), Melanie B. either does it outdoors at her Alberta farm or at a dog wash in Calgary. Housed in an old car wash building, the do-it-yourself grooming spot makes it easy by providing blow dryers, elevated tubs, grooming tables, and even waterproof aprons. "It saves my back from trying to remove all the hair and dirt from my tub," Melanie says. Many cities have fully loaded dog washes—with extras like ramps for older dogs and secure, flexible collar systems.

The Brush-Off

While most dogs prefer brushing to bathing, there are still many opportunities to go wrong or right. Plus there are as

If you wash your dog in your own shower or tub, Melanie says, remember a hair snare. Self-sealing, flexible snares fit in a variety of drains and are designed especially for pets.

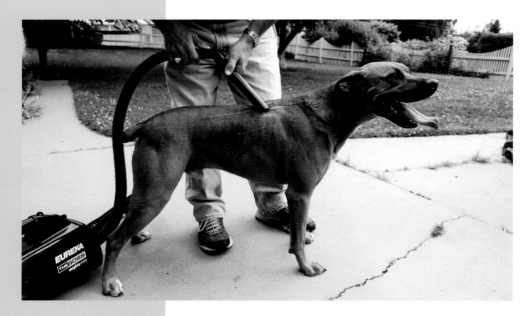

On cold days, don't forget about the garage for brushing. Indoors, a sheet on the floor reduces vacuuming time and saves bags.

When all else fails—as when your dog is blowing her undercoat and looks like she's spawning puppies—many folks swear by a professional groomers' high-velocity hair dryer, which blasts away heavy undercoat in a way you just can't do at home.

During heavy shedding season, Cindy Trimble Kelly uses a PetVac, a vacuum attachment designed for removing pet fur. It has a super-long hose, so you can leave the vacuum in the other room and the motor sound won't upset the dogs. She vacuums them when they are drying after the bath—since bathing promotes shedding.

many opinions on how best to brush a shedding dog as there are hairs on my couch. It really depends on your dog's coat and temperament and your patience and tolerance for fur.

Select the right tools.

There is no one-size-fits-all tool. All you have to do is think about the difference between a bichon frise, a poodle, and a Lab to understand why. But some brushing tools come up again and again as favorites:

- Deshedding tools designed to remove loose under-coat, such as those made by Furminator
- Currycombs and shedding blades, which are typically used for grooming cattle and horses
- Metal flea-control combs

Location is everything.

Not everybody can brush their dogs outside. Amy Lerma brushes her German shepherd, King, in any room in the house, but vacuums immediately after she's finished. Her recent in-sight was to spray a coat conditioner, just before brushing King. She says the damp fur doesn't fly away and land on everything in the room, making cleanup easier. Since not all dogs like the sound of a spray or the feeling of the mist, she recommends being extra patient and having treats at the ready.

Pedicures

Perhaps there is no more potentially traumatic grooming chal-lenge than clipping your dogs' nails. Many dogs won't stand for it. They don't like the snap of the clippers and probably sense our anxiety over the operation. What we most fear is cutting the quick—the fleshy interior of the nail—causing our dog pain and drawing blood.

- *Touchy-feely is good.* Even before you think of trimming your dog's nails, get him or her used to being touched all over, especially on the paws. It's an important part of making all grooming, especially nail trimming, easier.
- *Nails first.* For bath-phobic dogs, trim nails first, and then hit the bath. The freshly bathed the dog is all fired up and anxious for the groomer's greatest challenge. Also, don't be stingy with rewards—treats, toys, games, or loving.
- *File?* Claudine Randazzo's rescue dog, Chance, has nails that splinter, so Claudine files them with an emery board. "Chance will lie there like she is getting a pedicure," she says.
- *Polish?* Obviously, this is strictly nonessential, but surprisingly, painted nails have their place. Texan Mandy Hall painted the toenails of her Great Dane silver. Why? Because Simon is a therapy dog working with children. He's big and can be a little intimidating. Funny toenails help put the children at ease.

Let it fly. Don't fret too much about flyaway fur during your backyard grooming sessions. Some folks like to let it float on the breeze so birds can weave it into their nests.

Save and spin. There are spinners out there who transform fur balls into beautiful—and sentimental—yarn, scarves, mittens, and even afghans (see "Dream Weaver").

DREAM WEAVER

For Detta Juusola, dog fur is no different from wool, mohair, or angora. "It's just another fiber," she says. But after spinning the fur of man's best friend into yarn for twenty-five years, she is used to some skepticism.

Detta learned to spin with regular wool, but incorporated dog fur almost right away—combining her new skill with a lifelong love of dogs. Early on, she wanted to spin a variety of fur, so she put an ad in the Sunday paper seeking clippings or brushings from specific breeds so she could learn the differences. Looking back, she thinks there were probably several people who thought she was a little nuts.

Eventually, Detta brought her samples to a dog show. Although no one bought anything, her brochure generated business. "I got calls for two years," she says. She realized that most people want something from their own dog.

Since then she's spun and knitted sweaters, mittens, scarves, and afghans. Sometimes folks just want the yarn, so they can knit something themselves. In general, Detta recommends blending dog fur with wool about 50/50 to add spring and strength to the yarn. An afghan that is half wool requires about two-and-a-half grocery bags of fur.

She loves the work, but warns it's not a good wage. It sounds like a lot when a pair of custom mittens costs one hundred dollars, but a spinner will put eight to ten hours into transforming Fido's fur into the fuzzy hand warmers.

Many people spin the fur to create a tactile keepsake. About a year before her Newfoundland, Tugboat, died, she knitted a scarf from his fur. "Every time I wear it I think, 'Oh, Tubby,'" she says. "It's like laying your cheek against the dog's cheek."

If you save your dog's fur, leave the bag open after collecting it until you feel any moisture is gone. You can save fur forever, as long as the moths don't get to it.

Nora Boyd in Iowa invested in a muzzle for trimming her Pembroke corgi's nails, because Gryphon could get vicious at nail time. "He really doesn't mind the muzzle much at all," she says. "He sees it, and realizes he's been beat, I think."

Nora eventually switched to a Dremel. "It's pretty hard to mess up with the Dremel if you're careful," she says, although it took nearly two months to do a full nail trim. She does have a warning: Make sure to tie your hair back. It can get wrapped around the spinning part.

If fish is the main ingredient in your dog's food, that may be what's cramping your kissy-face style.

Those guys in shop were on to something.
Some people use a small Dremel sander to grind down the nail. For those of us who failed shop, a Dremel is a small motorized sanding wheel, usually used for woodcraft projects.

Kevin N. in Prescott, Arizona, learned about the Dremel from his basenji's breeder and says that, with some effort, it's worked like a charm for several dogs. But it requires patience. He recommends a systematic, slow introduction.

With his chow chow mix, Grizzley Ralph, Kevin took his time. One day, he just showed Grizz the sander. Then he let Grizz sniff it (and probably lick it) for a few minutes, while Kevin made happy talk: "Lookie, pup. We get to do your NAILS!!!" He was upbeat and ended the introduction with a treat. A couple of days later, another introduction and treat. Another day with the sander on, more happy talk and treats.

Eventually, Kevin sanded just one nail very quickly—not worrying about getting it as short as possible. Then he heaped on the praise, pets, and a cookie. It wasn't long before Grizz thumped his tail at the mere sight of the Dremel, because it meant Kevin had a cookie in his pocket with Grizz's name on it.

Kevin's working with Abby now, a malamute–Lab mix he adopted from a shelter. It's been an even slower go because she was abused before winding up at the pound and will not tolerate anyone touching her feet, much less holding on to them. Still Kevin thinks the sander will be better than a nail clipper, where one bad cut can set things back a long time. Many of Kevin's suggestions will work well for introducing a nail clipper as well.

Other Grooming Boondoggles

The loveliest dog in the world loses her luster when her breath peels paint, and an oozing hot spot is almost as painful to behold as it is to endure. So let's beat these recurring challenges with dog-park smarts.

Sweeten doggie breath.
Halitosis doesn't have to ruin your cuddle sessions with your dog. Clean teeth and healthy gums are essential in combating unsavory breath. Canine toothbrushes, poultry-flavored toothpaste (yum!), and dental cleansing pads and sponges help and are also important tools for fighting gum disease, which particularly affects small dogs. (Chew toys with nubs are also good for massaging gums.) In addition, popular breath-freshening shortcuts include these:

- Mint and charcoal dog biscuits
- Dental chews (a huge variety is available)
- Papaya

THE RELUCTANT DOG SHAMPOO ENTREPRENEUR

When Scout, Alisa Puga-Keesey's Rhodesian ridgeback puppy, first arrived in northern Uganda for a four-month stay in 1995, he must have thought he'd died and gone to heaven. While Alisa visited rural families for a nonprofit group that developed low-cost innovations to improve food and economic security, Scout roamed free in the African bush, investigating the wild and unfamiliar landscape.

Unfortunately, as a result of his exotic rambles and exposure to Sub-Saharan fleas and ticks, Scout developed a chronic itch, painful sores, and hot spots.

"It was the saddest thing," Alisa says. "My dog was so miserable."

In a fortuitous convergence of circumstances, Alisa turned to shea butter. She'd spent years teaching rural women in Uganda how to process shea nuts with maize grinders to create a premium butter for export and use in cosmetics. She knew all about shea butter's skin-healing properties. Desperate, she slathered the cold-press butter on Scout. Within days, his condition improved. Eventually, he stopped scratching completely.

"I used to joke with my friends that I'd make shea products for dogs," Alisa says. But as an anthropologist, it took a little while to see that pet shampoo might be her future. So, with a happier pup at her side, she continued what she started, working with the Cooperative Office for Voluntary Organizations and the Shea Project for Land Conservation and Development.

After September 11, 2001, funding dried up. Back in Santa Cruz, Alisa and her anthropologist husband, Jon, turned their energies toward building a sustainable, fair-trade market for shea producers. In a Berkeley lab, they transformed her experience with Scout into a full line of therapeutic shea butter shampoos, conditioners, tonics, and balms. Enhanced with essential oils and antioxidants, SheaPet products promote a healthy coat and help relieve and control common canine skin conditions.

When Alisa returns to Uganda, locals still ask about Scout, who died in 2007. Despite a cultural difference in attitudes toward dogs and Scout's tendency to push women off their mats so he wouldn't have to sit in the mud, he became an important figure in the community, Alisa explains. He was even the subject of prophecy. "The locals had dreams that the rebels came in the middle of the night and Scout rescued them."

If your dog chews on rope or fleecy toys, check his or her teeth regularly, says Barbara Teigen from Nashotah, Wisconsin. When her dachshund, Eugene U Genius, developed bad breath, she investigated and discovered "fleecy, ropy stuff" caught in his teeth. "I even tried dental floss to get that gunk out of there. It worked. Kinda," she says. "He wasn't crazy about it! I put a retrieving dumbbell in his mouth to keep his jaws open enough to work on the teeth with the floss. It helped that my son held him steady." Once Eugene's teeth were clean, no more stinky breath.

Take the sizzle out of hot spots.
Kate Rogers kept a small tin of Bag Balm on hand for her husky mix, Denali. Bag Balm salve was created for soothing irritated cow's udders and became popular for treating the chapped feet and hands of people. "My mom put little tins in our Christmas stockings one year," Kate

says. "I decided to try it on the dog." She found that even when Denali licked some of it off, it still worked wonders on hot spots.

Martha E., who lives in Mississippi, where they put the "hot" in hot spot, discovered that using Dermoplast (an antibacterial pain-relieving spray in a red can) helps hot spots heal fairly quickly. It should be noted, however, that it has not been tested or approved for dogs.

At the Park

PEOPLE, LIKE DOGS, ARE REALLY PACK ANIMALS. For most of us, living with *Canis familiaris* isn't an escape from *Homo sapiens*. There are some exceptions—misanthropes holed up in compounds waiting for the End Times in the company of several dozen hounds, for example. But generally, dogs provide opportunities to connect with other people. Two leashed pups sniffing each other on the street form a link between strangers. At play dates or the dog park, off-leash dogs gambol and cavort while their people look on like parents and talk about diets and obedience challenges.

Loving our dogs leads us into all sorts of entanglements—such as joining activist groups and volunteering for organizations—on their behalf. Plus there's a rapidly expanding online universe, the virtual dog parks, in the form of social networking sites, forums, groups, and blogs that allow us to talk about, question, praise, and explore our lives with dogs 24/7.

In this chapter, we fetch some advice for getting the most out of your actual, for-real dog park as well as some of the finer points of dog-fueled communities (including groups of two) from the folks who've been there, done that.

LEASH-FREE ETIQUETTE

We've come a long way from the days of unenforced leash laws, through crackdowns, to carving out designated spaces for dogs to play off-leash. Today, many municipalities have off-leash zones. Developers are adding dog parks to retirement communities and the rooftops of condo complexes. So, more and more, we enjoy the opportunities and face the challenges of letting our dog romp leash-free with other dogs.

No two off-leash areas (OLAs) are the same. In New York City, certain sections of the eighty-eight parks, including Central Park, are designated off-leash areas from 6 AM to 9 AM and 9 PM to midnight. In addition, more than fifty and counting fenced dog runs (some with pools) dot the city. In the Seattle area, there are more than a dozen OLAs that range from forty partially fenced acres with a river to a fully fenced urban lot. Boulder, Colorado, has fenced off-leash areas for well-behaved dogs plus swaths of mountainous open space where dogs who qualified for voice and sight control tags can romp leash-free.

No single set of rules can apply to such a variety of circumstances, but there are some baseline codes of conduct that park users and stewards pretty much agree on.

Exercise common sense and other OLA Dos.

- Do bring well-trained dogs who get along with other dogs and people, respond to voice control, and can use the dog parks responsibly.

- Stop bothersome dog behavior immediately.
- Scoop your own dog's poop as well as waste "accidentally" left behind by others.
- Focus on your dog.
- Carry a leash and extra waste bags.
- Be prepared to end your visit if your dog is causing problems.
- Bring water for your pup if there isn't a supply at the park.
- Close and latch any gates behind you.

ixNay on the icnicpay and other OLA Don'ts.
- Leave food at home. Snacking and picnicking at the park inspires bad behavior. Some stewards even advise against bringing dog treats, but that seems unrealistic, especially for guardians who are using treats to train their dogs in the off-leash area.
- Don't let your dogs dig. Digging runs down the park and creates leg-breaking hazards. If your paw-pal loves to excavate, create a sandbox for her at home.
- Don't hang out near the entrance, where altercations can break out with excited new arrivals.
- No naked dogs, that is, no dogs without collars, ID, license, and rabies tags.
- No spike, prong, or pinch collars.

Bite-and-run is not allowed.

In most New York City dog runs, you'll be reminded at the entry gate that you are financially liable for any injury caused by your dog. You will also be asked politely to settle all vet bills with the owner before visiting the run again. If your dog gets into a fight, exchange contact information and leave. (This is actually in the fine print of most dog-park rules.)

Garrett Rosso, the manager of the Tompkins Square Dog Run in New York City's East Village, says, "This is the friggin' most important rule." It's a rule born out of economic reality. While a stitch and a drain once cost about two hundred dollars in Manhattan, today it's closer to two thousand dollars. And don't think you can get away without paying. "There is a dog-run newsgroup where everyone gets on and gossips and, god forbid you don't pay your bill," Garrett says. "We monitor each other like crazy."

Respect neutered territory.
It's a good idea to neuter your dog. Intact dogs are more likely to be attacked or to provoke aggression. (We're not talking about puppies.) Bitches in heat are equally problematic.

There's no such thing as too much bling.
"To anybody who says, 'My dog stays with me and he'll never run off,' I say, 'Until it happens,'" says Judy Trockel, the chief bottle washer at the forty-two-acre Marymoor Park dog park in Redmond, Washington. Dogs in an off-leash area are at more risk to run off or go free—especially in unfenced areas—and a spooked dog moves quickly. Judy has seen it happen. She says collars should have legible, up-to-date contact information, plus a vet tag and a pet license. (She suggests using your cell phone number on tags, so you can be reached as soon as someone finds your dog.) Microchipping is also recommended.

Don't use chain, choke, or prong collars.
Without a leash attached, chain, choke, and prong collars serve no purpose and cause serious problems when dogs wrestle. The collars can become linked, freaking out the dogs. Dogs can

For some dogs, collars cause fur loss or irritation around the neck. One innovative solution is to wrap your dog's collar in soft fleece. Horse supply shops sell fleece halter covers, which are essentially tubes with a Velcro closure. They protect the horse's cheeks, crown, and muzzle. These covers can be cut to work as a collar wrap.

If your dog is the Imelda Marcos of collars, buy a removable tag holder, which makes it easy to snap your dog's license, rabies tag, and ID to any collar. Some off-leash areas require licenses and are patrolled. Don't get caught empty collared.

get their jaws caught in the prongs or their teeth lodged in one of the chains. One member of the National Dog Run news list almost lost a finger trying to break up a fight with a dog in a prong collar. Other users have seen serious, even lethal consequences for dogs.

What about on-leash in the off-leash area?
"If the run isn't very crowded and people seem amenable, a dog that is undergoing training can be safely leashed in the dog run," says Tod Wohlfarth, co-chair of NYCdog Dog Park

Committee and president of Friends of Leroy Dog Run. "However, generally it is a serious party foul. The leash is essentially an accelerator for a dog's anxiety when it feels threatened."

There is usually no great reason to bring leashed dogs into an off-leash area. After all, there are plenty of places to leash-walk a dog. Sometimes it's just a temporary measure to get your dog into the park or out of a bad situation or so he or she doesn't bolt to an open gate. If you need to have a leashed dog in the off-leash area (and it's permitted), don't use the extension-type leads. Dogs can be hurt in tangles, and some DPW tipsters have seen rushing dogs clotheslined by an extended, taut line.

Wolves, Dumpers, Humpers, and Jerks

There are some situations not covered in basic codes of dog-park conduct. These are the more subtle issues of etiquette that seem to have less to do with dog obedience than the interpersonal skills of the people.

Wolves. Like the wild critters from which they descended, these dogs crisscross the park or the pond seeking out balls missed or dropped by slower, less vigilant retrievers. You can't blame them for doing their job. If you're playing fetch with a chronic ball dropper, keep your eye on her. You can also label the ball, bring an unusual ball that stands out in the sea of Penns and Dunlops, or bring backups. Remember, dog parks are ball graveyards. Don't get hung up on a particular ball—you're bound to sprain your ankle on another soon.

Does it need to be said? No dogs with communicable diseases or infections.

If your dog brings you a slimy prize and you have no idea who the owner is, make a good faith effort—holding the tattered ball aloft with a "This belong to anyone?" will suffice. "What you bring into the run becomes community property, period," Tod Wohlfarth says. "Further, special toys cause fights. Don't bring a fancy toy to the run, just a tennis ball. If your dog doesn't like tennis balls, tough caca."

Dumpers. You witness a dog pooping and the person in charge misses it. The proper response is *not* to assume the worst and bitch and moan to your companions or your dog about lame owners. Take the high road: Assume the best and offer a friendly point to the offending pile or ask the negligent owner if he needs a bag (always with a smile). Most people aren't blowing it off, and they appreciate being reminded. Better yet, just pick it up, earn some karma points, and move on.

If the offending party is on his or her cell phone, all bets are off. When people bring their dogs to the park and promptly ignore them—by dialing up the cell, reading the newspaper, or tuning out with a friend—it's called "dumping." It's a big no-no. Many off-leash areas actually have rules against jabbering on the cell phone in the park. This is not the case at the Tompkins Square Dog Run. As Garrett says, "You're just not going to put up a No Cell Phones rule in New York City."

Humpers. Mounting is a chronic complaint for some and an embarrassment for others. Some guardians just don't think it's a big deal. (Man: "He's a chip off the old block." Woman: "He never does this.") While not all dogs mount as a prelude to an orgy of violence, things do go awry.

The bottom line is that humping equals big deal if the humpee or the guardian of the humpee thinks it's a big deal. It comes down to respect. If I don't want my dog to be mounted—because she's old and she has bad hips or because it freaks me out—I should be able to say, "Please stop your dog." And that should be the end of it. But that's not always the end of it.

Jerks. Judy Trockel puts the jerk share of the population at about 3 percent. The same holds true for off-leash areas. "It's the 3 percent theory," Judy says. "Some people say, 'Only 3 percent?'"

Once you accept that there are jerks out there, you stop expecting perfection in your fellow attendees and learn avoidance. Don't get into verbal confrontations. "The number-one skill that I tell people to use at the dog park is to move on," Judy says. If you have deemed another regular user to be a jerk, avoid him or her. Recognize that not all dogs get along, nor do all people.

Navigating the Human Factor

Dog parks are not only good socialization for dogs, but they're also good for us. There aren't that many environments where people of such diverse backgrounds, ethnicities, and socio-economic groups have something in common. If we're lucky, we make friends.

Still, for some of us, it's the people that are the hitch. As in high school, there are cliques at the parks—pros, regulars, breed groups, loners, nerds. So follow your dog's lead. No, don't start trouser sniffing, but a little human congress will enhance your experience and put your dogs at ease.

Say hello. It won't hurt you. Remember, humans have names, too. I'm learning to introduce myself along with my dog. After a while, it's weird to know the full health history of Jack, Pepper, Scout, Little Mac, and Gracie and not know the name of the person at the other end of the leash.

Bring a business card. If you're looking for ideal playmates for your pup, don't be caught empty handed, especially if you've got a choosy dog. When your dog meets another who brings out his playtime spirit, you might want to set up future meetings. Bring a card with your contact information (maybe something with your dog's adorable mug), and you won't miss out on a chance to reconnoiter another day.

Enjoy the human behavior lab. Just as you can study animal behavior, the dog park is a place to study human behavior. "There is something about being in a dog park, surrounded by so many excited, primal energies, that overrides many social inhibitions," Tod Wohlfarth says. "We've had people come in and open up the gates to free the dogs. I've had an elderly man with a puppy threaten another elderly widow with bodily harm because her dog was playing too 'roughly' with his new puppy. It goes on and on like that.

"On the flip side, I've met the most wonderful people at the park," Tod continues, "many of whom become fast friends and assist each other not only with each other's dogs but with their lives as well."

TRICKED OUT AND READY TO THROW

There's more to the dog park than dogs. Regulars know that certain supplies are the difference between a walk in the park and a romp.

Wear a belt.

Learn the lesson of "Duke" at the Laurel Canyon off-leash park in Los Angeles. I didn't catch his name (my bad) but I remember he was wearing a Duke University T-shirt. He walks Tank (see, I know the dog's name), a very sweet bulldog with a bit of a jumping problem. One day, Tank jumped on Duke, whose sweatpants had no drawstring, pantsing him. Takeaway: Even if your dog isn't a jumper, another dog might be. Be sure you have a strong waistband, belt, or suspenders.

Bring supplies.

Judy Trockel takes a tote bag into the park with her. She carries extra plastic bags, extra balls, a leash, her wallet, zip ties (in case she sees a hole in the fence), clippers (in case blackberries have grown over the path), her cell phone (for emergencies), a couple of pens, and a pad of paper. If she sees a conflict, she can help people exchange their information. She might also write down a new friend's name and number.

Unretire your passport holder.

Forget about cumbersome, ugly fanny packs. Joyce Gehl, an artist with an eye for style, carries supplies for her poodle, Rocky, in a passport holder. In the lightweight nylon pouch, which she can wear around her neck or waist, she squirrels away a few folded plastic bags and treats. If she's heading to a park, she clips a small mesh bag with Rocky's tennis ball to the holder.

Make a treat rattle.

In addition to her tote bag, Judy also carries treats in a plastic jar with a screw lid. This is for Boogie, her nineteen-year-old beagle, who gets distracted. As long as she shakes his "cookie jar," he keeps following her. She doesn't like to carry treats in her pocket because scent dogs will smell them and wander over.

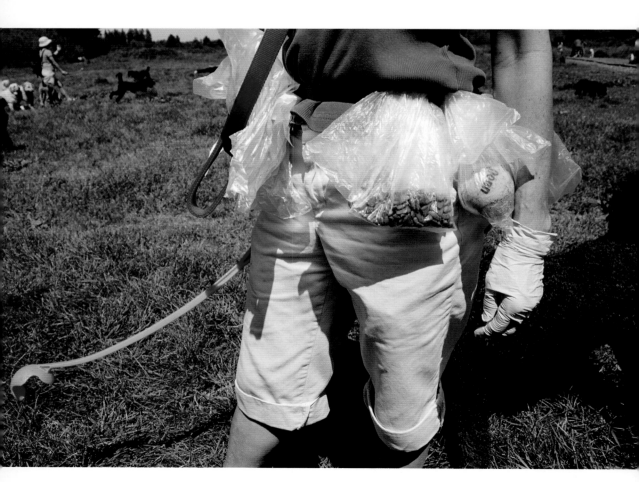

Consider these better ball options.

While it makes visual sense for your soccer dog to nose-dribble the old black-and-white classic, the leather skin of soccer balls is easily punctured, torn, and swallowed. Dani Baker uses a small, tough-skinned basketball for her soccer-mad dachshund.

If you play fetch after dark, pretty common in the northern latitudes where I live, a glow-in-the-dark ball can be a major asset, especially if your retriever is easily distracted.

What about retrieving bumpers? These have long been used for training bird dogs, and now they are showing up at dog beaches. A short lanyard increases throwing distances. A long lanyard makes the bumper more easily retrievable when pups-in-training get distracted.

Roll your own.

I've found that in a pinch my clean newspaper poop bag can double as a water bowl. Just roll down the sides to create a basin and fill it from a park water fountain. For some reason, people are irritated if you let your dog drink directly from the fountain.

Towel up.

On hot days, resourceful types drape towels across their car's front windshield to keep the front seat cool, and they're prepared for wiping down wet, muddy dogs after playtime.

Never give a treat to someone else's dog without asking the owner first—that goes for the lady in my neighborhood who keeps giving biscuits to my weight-watching hound against my express wishes.

FUR-FREE KIDS IN FUR BABY'S PLAYGROUND

Children in a dog park? Dog people come down on all sides of this question. Some off-leash areas discourage or prohibit young children in the dog area. Others set age limits and/or require that children be seated most of the time. It's true that toddlers can get into all kinds of trouble, especially if they are unattended and start running around.

That said, an OLA can be a great environment for well-behaved, well-managed children (just like the dogs). It can be a good place to get them accustomed to dogs, and it can help them develop an appreciation for the dog park. "I look at the kids as our volunteers of the future," says Judy Trockel, who volunteers her time at a large OLA near her home. Still, adults need to do their reconnaissance to know the scene (every OLA has a different atmosphere, level of intensity, and mix of people and pups) and prep their children on how to act in this setting.

Remember, many dogs aren't used to being around firecracker kids. Loud noise and quick movements can frighten them. They may chase, jump on, or even nip rushing kids, just like they would another dog. Children should never touch or feed a strange dog without talking to the guardian.

HOW TO GET MORE OUT OF YOUR DOG PARK

If you or your dog have never been to the off-leash park, here's some advice from wily veterans.

- Go at a time when the park isn't so crowded.
- Keep your first visit short, sweet, and positive.
- If your dog is acting stressed out, take him home immediately.
- Worried your dog's a bolter? Be sure the OLA is fully fenced.
- Consider visiting without your dog the first time. Walk around and talk to the users.

Time your visits.

If you want your dog to have lots of pals with whom to romp, find out when the dog walkers come—usually late mornings when the nine-to-fivers are nine-to-fiving.

Also, since not all OLAs have good shade trees or shelters, during hotter months non-pros tend to congregate early morning and late evening, or when tree shade reaches the dog park.

Discover the advantages of small parks.

Folks often complain about pocket parks because they don't offer a lot of room to run and at peak times things get crowded. However, Seattle pet portraitist Jamie Pflughoeft found that a fenced, urban pocket park was ideal for training her adopted ridgeback, Fergie. In the small, controlled environment, she knew she'd never lose sight of her pup. Intensive training is another way to entertain and tire your dog.

Wear dog-park clothes.

So you don't worry about getting filthy.

Become an active observer.

OLAs are laboratories of pack animal behavior. If you pay attention to your dog, you can learn a lot. How does your pet respond to a charging dog? A fleeing dog? A group blocking the trail?

Is he or she sensitive to any particular breeds or behaviors? Use this opportunity to develop a better understanding of your dog.

At her local OLA, Mountaineers Books editor Kate Rogers learned that her husky–Lab mix, Denali, had a thing for Great Danes. "She mostly ignored other dogs, making a beeline along the trail, with the occasional stop-and-sniff along the way," Kate says. "But if she saw a Dane, Denali would always approach him or her and try to engage." Once Kate realized it, she tried to create more opportunities for play with these gentle giants. She also discovered Denali was more likely to swim when fewer dogs were on the beach and that she perked up in grassy areas. Kate drove a little farther to an OLA with meadows. "These are all small things, but they went a long way to deepening my care for her," Kate says.

Be prepared.
"Every dog has their thing that they do at the park to embarrass their owner," says Seattleite Michelle Goodman, whose dog, Buddy, has a rep as a ball thief. "You need to know what you are going to do about it beforehand and come with ammo you need."

Take Garrett Rosso's advice for small, crowded dog runs. Come to the park when your dog is in control. How do you know she's in control? She's not pulling you down the path to the park. Come after a forty-five-minute walk, when she's relaxed. When you can put her in a stay, open the gate, walk in. If

Join your park's volunteer steward group, if there is one. Get involved, even if you just donate money. The more you put in, the more you'll get out.

Many OLAs are overcrowded or hard to reach. If you live in an underserved community, start a new off-leash area. Contact the nearest OLA organization and they'll help you get started.

she doesn't follow until you call—that's when you know your dog is ready for the dog park. Stay for fifteen to twenty minutes. Leave on a pleasant note.

Practice recall.

Keep your dog's recall skills sharp by practicing recall at the park with lots of treats and a far remove from the exit. "Don't make the only time you call your dog be when you are getting ready to leave," says Laura Jean Rathmann, who helped create off-leash areas in St. Paul and Ramsey County, Minnesota. She also suggests practicing play exits and giving lots of treats when you circle near double gates, so dogs associate the park exit with good things.

DOG PARK DATING

The dog park is hot for singles, dating expert Diane Mapes says. While parks can't compete with the Internet, for dog lovers those open spaces are better than a singles bar—with dog lounges and dog-centric mixers close behind.

The author of two books about dating, including *How to Date in the Post-Dating World*, Diane does not have a dog of her own. But she loves dogs and has seen them work their magic for lonely hearts, including two friends who met online. With two dogs apiece, they both put a premium on dog love and their first date was walking all four together. Before long, Diane was playing the accordion at their wedding.

"Dogs are a safe icebreaking topic, which a lot of times is all you need," Diane explains. Ask about toys, collars, breed, and health issues, she says. "You can also set your dog after somebody. You know, 'Sic 'em.' And then you're all 'I'm so sorry. She's never jumped up on anyone like that before. Here, let me brush that dust off your fine-tuned, muscley pectorals.' They can be a great wing man for you."

Did I mention Diane doesn't actually have a dog?

Still, she's right. With a dog you often don't have to start the conversation, and many a tongue-tied hunk or hunkette finds voice at the sight of a fuzzy, flop-eared sidekick.

Four-pawed pals are excellent judges of character, even when we aren't. "Dogs can be very helpful in separating the wheat from the chaff," Seattle dating maven Diane Mapes says. When she heard author and creepy person–expert Ann Rule speak, Rule gave the women in the audience this advice: If you're going out with somebody, don't introduce him to your friends or your family, introduce him to your dog. When Rule worked at a crisis center in Seattle with serial killer Ted Bundy (before his brutal spree), he charmed everyone except Rule's dog. She told the crowd that her pup growled, his hackles went up, and his ears went back every time he saw Bundy.

First-Date Tips

A first date is rarely easy, and bringing along seventy-five pounds of alpha will complicate matters. A few simple pointers (and I don't mean of the German shorthaired pointer variety) can grease the wheels of this potentially awkward rendezvous.

> Make puppy introductions on
> neutral ground.

This is essential for dogs who give out the old *dis-here'z-me-wumun* vibe.

> A few rolls of the lint brush are not
> out of order.

In collecting dating disaster stories, Diane learned about a woman who picked up her first date in a fur-covered car. "She hadn't done any kind of precleaning at all," Diane says. "The shoulder strap on his side was chewed all the way through, and even though he liked dogs, this was a problem for him."

> Wait to spill all the beans.

"Maybe you don't want to tell your date that you do the full-body spoon with your dog until you're sure that that's cool," Michelle Goodman says. "You know, the same way you wait to reveal that you have the full bondage kit. Hopefully, you're going to suss them out and see if they are on the same page."

> Listen and learn.

If someone says they don't like dogs, and he or she has potential otherwise, don't just dismiss them out of hand. "They may have had some trauma, which is why they don't like dogs, and it's not that they are a horrible, uncaring person," Diane says. "Maybe there is room for growth there."

Online Options

Like everything else, online dating has gone to the dogs. Niche dating sites, such as *www.datemypet.com*, *www.animalattraction.com*, and *www.doglover.biz*, promise to connect animal lovers with one another. If you want to cast your line in a more populated pond, such as *www.eharmony.com*, *www.match.com*, or newspaper personals, state your dog passion upfront. Not only will this attract like-minded folks, it filters out prospects like Michael Vick.

THE SEARCH FOR LOVE

There are several times in *A Dog's Life: A Dogamentary*, when Emmy Award-winning filmmaker Gayle Kirschenbaum starts up conversations with strange men on the streets of New York City. (Not strange as in talking-to-lampposts, but strange as in unfamiliar.) She explains that her Shi Tzu is looking for love. Sometimes she's more direct about seeking a match for herself. The guys never seem to mind. There's something about the silky dog with a camera strapped to her back—filming from her own doggie point of view—that makes the whole situation nonthreatening.

When Gayle adopted Chelsea more than a decade ago, it was, she says, "mutual rescue." Since then, she has taken her "dogter," sometimes sporting heart-shaped sunglasses and a pink visor, everywhere. It was probably unavoidable that Chelsea would end up a star.

Although *A Dog's Life* was originally planned as a sort of *Sex and the City* meets *Best in Show*, filming and life took a serious turn on September 11, 2001. Gayle was out shooting morning scenes with Chelsea on the Lower West Side when she witnessed and even managed to film some of that day's tragedy and heartbreak. At one point, a confused worker from downtown asked Gayle if she could pet Chelsea—saying it was the best thing she'd seen all day.

Gayle immediately followed up on an old desire to volunteer with Chelsea as a therapy dog. "It took 9/11 to get me to get her signed up right away," Gayle says. "We wanted to help immediately." From September through January, they worked at a makeshift assistance center for families and friends of victims. When it closed,

Gayle and Chelsea shifted their work to St. Vincent's Hospital in the West Village and later to Cabrini hospice.

Eventually, Gayle picked up her camera again. But this time, she filmed Chelsea at work, spreading her dog love among terminally ill patients. One visit didn't make it onto film. A woman Gayle had not met asked if Chelsea would visit her mother. Chelsea clearly wanted to go to the sleeping woman, but when Gayle set her on the bed, the dog began to bark in a dramatic break from her standard practice. When the patient opened her eyes, her daughter started to cry and a representative from the pet therapy program ran out of the room to call in the staff. What Gayle didn't know until that moment was the patient had been in a coma and was expected to die without coming out of it.

While not every visit was so monumental, many of them enriched the lives of everyone involved. The irony is not lost on this filmmaker and story teller—that a project begun as a light-hearted search for a pair of Mr. Rights ended with the discovery of love in a very different place.

TIME TO W-A-L-K

Peter Kunz, a professional dog walker in New York City (see "Dream Job: Dog Walker"), offers these suggestions for nurturing a positive dog-walking experience with your own pup.

- *Watch:* "This is what I tell my customers: Watch your dog," Peter says. "Observe them, watch their body language, and you will learn about their needs and how to treat your pup the right way."
- *Don't tense up:* "I would love it if dog owners were more relaxed when they saw another dog on a leash," Peter says. Most dogs just want to check each other out. "People should trust their own dog and loosen the leash and try."
- *Seek shade and quiet:* In New York, this means avoiding the avenues and taking the side streets, which, in the summer, is also where you'll find shade. Avoid loud noises, such as jackhammers. "Walk the way you want to walk when you want to walk in peace," Peter says.
- *Talk to your dog:* Sit on a bench. Pet the dog. Talk to him. Peter looks the dog in the eye and tells him about his day, his shopping list, whatever is on his mind. "This is what makes a dog trust in you," he says. Plus, it helps Peter let go of his stories.
- *Take breaks:* Most dogs don't need to run at full tilt for a full hour. Peter gives them time to do other things, such as stand around, sniff, walk, and stare. He believes letting them follow their own muse makes them happier and healthier.

To learn about therapy dog training, contact the Delta Society (*www.deltasociety.org*).

Run errands with your dog: Joyce Gehl works above Pike Place Market in Seattle, and she brings her black standard poodle, Rocky, to her studio-office. Many days during her lunch break, she and Rocky walk through the market doing errands. Joyce is known as the "Poodle Lady" by some regulars, and she's even permitted to bring Rocky into the Italian market where she gets her espresso. Meanwhile, Rocky has canine friends he can visit in a number of boutiques while Joyce shops or browses.

Foul weather cozies: Pop a towel in the dryer before walking on cold, wet days. Wrap your chilly partner in the warming, drying goodness as soon as you get home.

DREAM JOB: DOG WALKER

Perhaps the most ubiquitous and long-standing job of the burgeoning new dog economy is dog walking. Walkers with one, two, even ten dogs are everywhere. Some are trainers and groomers and vet techs, but many more are refugees from fur-free careers. They are former bartenders and landscapers, software designers and mechanics, empty nesters and recent graduates. They do it for the fresh air, to be their own boss, because they love dogs, and because the money's decent. Yes, you can make a living, and a good one, as a professional dog perambulator. But it's not easy.

Peter Kunz has been walking dogs for four years in the dog walker's Mecca: New York City. From his first memory—two Dobermans peering into his crib—to growing up in Switzerland with off-leash canines of all types, dogs have been a major part of his life. But he never expected they'd lead to work. An advertising copywriter, Kunz continues his "day job" even as he walks more than thirty dogs with the help of two other walkers.

His approach is one-on-one. He does not walk more than one dog at a time nor does he take groups for supervised off-leash play. "I'm not fooling around," Peter says in soothing, Swiss-accented English. "I'm not in it for the money. I do it because I really love dogs." He's read plenty of training books but he says he's guided by intuition, which leads to some unorthodox moves such as sleeping on the floor with dogs during overnight pet-sitting gigs.

For Peter, walking a dog is about much more than exercise. It's about studying the behaviors of city dogs and also forging a bond.

When Walkies Aren't Enough

Walking simply isn't enough of a workout for Aaron Wiehe's white husky, Nisha. So he attaches a standard leash to her harness and lets her pull him on his skateboard. If it's raining, he brings an umbrella. There are also leash contraptions for cycling with a dog (called bike-joring). Just remember dogs wear out faster than most riders.

Running does the trick for Dave Swenson, an economics researcher in Ames, Iowa. Miss Daisy One Dot, a rat terrier, joins Dave at the end of a five-foot leash on long runs.

"I trained her just like I would a marathon runner," he says. "We started easy. We got her feet strong. We slowly increased her distance until doing a ten- to fifteen-mile weekend run is her norm. She likes that."

She has twice completed the Wyoming Marathon and the Central States Marathon—winning as the sole canine entry every time. In 2007, she finished the Fat Ass 50K (thirty-one miles) in Cameron, Missouri, and the Rockin' K Trail Marathon near Ellsworth, Kansas.

He always brings an old swimming cap and a water bottle. "It's easy and it's cheap and it just tucks right into your waist," he says about his makeshift bowl. If Daisy gets too hot, Dave pours water all over her and rubs it in. "It's just like turbo-charging her. You cool a dog down, it's just like lighting a rocket up their butt."

BEYOND THE WOOD CHIPS

Dog parks are a particular kind of canine-human society. Egalitarian and spontaneous, they don't work for all dogs or all people. More and more guardians are seeking out structured opportunities where their dogs can play with others of the same breed, or size, or with shared passions, such as herding. These meetings are facilitated by a variety of clubs, organizations, websites, online forums, and day cares.

Training, classes, demos, and competitions in Earthdog, Schutzhund, lure course, confirmation, tracking, obedience, flygility, K9 drill team, musical freestyle, skijoring and sledding, dock diving, Doga (see "Dream Job: Doga Instructor"), agility, and more engage your dog's body and mind and cement your bond.

One way to sample a smorgasbord of possibilities is through Dog Scouts of America (DSA). Dog Scouts is a nonprofit organization dedicated to the idea that dogs and their people are happiest learning new skills and sports together. That's everything from pulling a sled and herding to geocaching and painting—regardless of the breed. Through DSA camps, outings, retreats, articles, newsletters, and a merit badge system (like the Boy Scouts, but way better), guardians and their dogs master new talents. They are also encouraged to engage in community service.

If you attend a yoga-with-dogs class, remember to bring your lint roller. Massage really causes the fur to fly all over your stretchy black yoga pants.

Playgroups

Wendy Hughes-Jelen was compelled to create a playgroup for Sophia, her skittish rescued Italian greyhound, when she discovered her pup was afraid of squeaky toys, tires, mud puddles, buses, cars, and other dogs.

She tried an unsuccessful one-on-one rendezvous with another Italian greyhound (set up through a breed listserv) at a small and shy dog off-leash area. Sophia spent the visit shivering in a bystander's lap. Nor did she get into the swing of a supervised puppy-playgroup dominated by terriers. And during a mixed-breed training class, an innocent lunge by a mastiff further curbed Sophia's taste for canine hobnobbing.

So Wendy, who had organized a Mini Cooper club through *www.meetup.com* a few years earlier, decided to try again. The website facilitates face time among like-minded people—and sometimes dogs—in dozens of cities. When she launched IGGY Ambassadors–Italian Greyhounds of the Northwest, she had thirty-five members in the first two days.

As guardians of Italian greyhounds (affectionately called Iggies) will tell you, the dogs generally like their own type. So their

people are happy to make small talk while the dogs chase each other and occasionally wrestle, standing on their back legs. The people may not know one another's names, but they speak the shared language of Iggy—finding common ground in the dogs' possessive and demanding temperament, high-maintenance requirements, elegance, and curiosity.

They meet about once a month at an indoor day care. On nice days, Wendy might announce an informal "pickup" meeting at an off-leash area. At least once a summer, she has hosted a picnic at her home. Last year, she had fifty dogs in her backyard. Here are five tried-and-true lessons from Wendy's Iggy potluck:

1. *Shore up your fencing.* Some guest dogs might be smaller than your dog and, in an unfamiliar and amped-up environment, may be more motivated to escape.

2. *Create a double gate, like the two-stage entry you see at dog parks.* Wendy set up an X-pen (flexible exercise pen) around the backyard gate to operate as a holding area between the backyard and the rest of the neighborhood. "You have to have that or you're going to lose someone," Wendy says.

3. *Keep any food out of reach.* Iggies may be small, but they know how to stand on their hind legs and steal hotdogs. Wendy raised her table on cinder blocks beyond the reach of the tallest pups. (Be warned: Adding food to a gathering of off-leash dogs increases difficulty.)

4. *Raise money for a good cause.* Wendy asked for a ten-dollar donation per person to raise money for Iggy rescue. In addition, she invites fellow group members who have Iggy-related businesses (such as a custom collar maker) to set up tables. So there is shopping.

5. *Mix it up.* Wendy invites friends and family to her Iggy picnic. She's found the antics of the dogs provide excellent entertainment for people who are unfamiliar with the breed.

Left to our own devices, we don't always take care of ourselves. Dogs give us an excuse to take up activities that are good for us, such as Doga and walking.

Virtual Dog Parks

Canine groups coming together via *www.meetup.com* are just one of the many spokes in the wheel of a modern dog's e-life. Today, our canine companions have their own web pages and email buddies, online personals, virtual packs, and playgroups. These social networks and forums are almost entirely virtual, with no actual sniffing. They include *www.mydogspace.com* and *www.dogstogether.com;* breed-centered forums such as *www.igpost.com* for Italian greyhound guardians; common interest groups on sites such as *www.nycdog.org;* rescue-related forums at *www.bestfriends.org* and *www.petfinder.com;* and on and on.

A MySpace-Friendster hybrid launched in early 2004, Dogster (*www.dogster.com*) is the big daddy of online dog communities, with hundreds of thousands of dogs. In many ways, it's a living, breathing, evolving dog park of the kind we mean when we talk about the free flow of dog park wisdom out there. Dogster members create profiles for their pups, post photos and videos, keep diaries, network, give and take advice in online forums, and join groups that sometimes even convene in real space and time. On Dogster, dogs do most of the talking. That means loads of BOL (bark out loud), "Praise Dog!" and jokes about p-mail and typing without opposable thumbs.

PAY IT FORWARD

Off-leash areas are one of several arenas in which we get our first taste of companion-animal volunteering and activism. We join clean-up days or sign a petition in support of a new dog park in an underserved area. Our relationships with our dogs lead us into varieties of knowledge—breed discrimination, overcrowded shelters, puppy mills, cruelty—that inspire action.

Many of the people I talked with for this book were typical dog lovers with full lives and no intention of signing on for more than the average train-feed-walk-play-snuggle routine. But sooner or later they were into a volunteer gig almost without realizing.

More than ten years ago, Petie Hoving got her first computer and started connecting with fellow miniature pinscher owners via a listserv she created. One fateful summer day, she received an email from someone looking to find a home for a "min-pin" puppy discovered in a hot garage. Even though it wasn't a rescue group, Petie and others at Internet Miniature Pinscher Services (IMPS, for short) leapt into action—finding volunteers and raising funds to transport the dog to a foster home and eventually a forever home. He was named Lister after the list.

"I thought that would be the end of it," Petie says. But the group answered an important need. Since 1998, IMPS has found homes for about 13,000 surrendered, abandoned, or otherwise unwanted miniature pinschers.

In her Manhattan apartment, Petie frequently dedicates as many as nine hours a day to the group she founded. At her side are her min-pins, Winston and Layla. The work has become a life saver. About five years ago, she was diagnosed with macular degeneration, and she has lost much of her sight. She can't see faces but with her computer screen set to enlarged type, she is able to receive and answer emails. Without the rescue, she says, "I'd be so bored. I'd be crawling the ceilings."

Frustrated by the number of strays in her hometown of Petersburg, Alaska, Anne Henshaw, a local dog groomer, teamed up with the town's only veterinarian to start a private shelter and affordable spay and neuter program. Today, there are very few unwanted dogs rolling into the shelter. When Anne winters near Puerto Vallarta in Mexico, she continues her efforts, volunteering at spay-neuter clinics in local villages and occasionally finding homes with friends in the States for abandoned dogs. Gayle Kirschenbaum, a filmmaker in New York City, trained her shih tzu, Chelsea, in animal-assisted therapy and volunteered to help families affected by 9/11 (see "The Search for Love"). It goes on and on—scratch the surface of a dog lover and you'll find a volunteer-in-waiting.

Just do it.

You don't have to start from scratch like Petie or Anne. Volunteer for a group or organization with which you already have a relationship. That's how most people get started. They walk dogs at the shelter where they adopted a dog. They clean up their own off-leash area. They train their pup for animal-assisted therapy at the hospice where a sick relative spent her last days.

There are also a variety of websites that connect wannabe volunteers with deserving organizations, including these:

- *www.volunteermatch.org* and *www.networkforgood.org* list animal-welfare gigs by location
- *www.charityguide.org* provides suggestions for making a difference on animal issues as an individual or as part of a group
- The Humane Society of the United States (*www.hsus.org*) provides a primer on how to volunteer at local animal shelters

Volunteer to help with grief.

"I tell volunteers who are experiencing grief to stay a little longer if they can," says Jeanne Modesitt, a longtime volunteer at Best Friends Animal Society, the largest no-kill sanctuary in the country. "I say really immerse yourself with these dogs because it is profoundly healing."

Five years ago, Jeanne, a children's book author, and her illustrator husband, Robin Spowart, were devastated by the death of their beloved Jack Russell–poodle mix, Bobo. They prayed for inspiration about how to cope—and an inner voice told them to go to Best Friends. The week they spent volunteering at the Utah sanctuary was so meaningful, they decided to move nearby from their home in New Mexico even before the week was over. "We both knew this was the place we needed to be in order to survive the death of our dog," Jeanne says.

Ask: Where am I most needed?

Jeanne also recommends that volunteers ask to work where the need is greatest. That question landed her and Robin, who both walk dogs four mornings a week, in an area at Best Friends called "the Lodges," for the difficult-to-place dogs, many of whom are dog-aggressive. "They are so happy to see us," Jeanne says. "It gives us such joy, we say, 'Our hearts are full of dog.'"

Be prepared for change.

After years of writing and illustrating books about bunnies and mice, Jeanne and Robin are now writing about and drawing the dogs they've met at Best Friends. "I just can't write about little bunnies anymore," Jeanne says. "Something about meeting these dogs has transformed us."

Take breaks.

Mary Kate McDermott, a Northwesterner who finds homes for St. Martin strays, takes a break from rescue work two to three months a year. "Everyone who is in any kind of rescue work hits that point. It's exhausting," she says. But she always wants back in. "That feeling of going to the airport and knowing where they've been, seeing how they've lived, and knowing what they are going to get here; it's just a euphoria."

Get educated and inspired and learn how to lobby at the annual Taking Action for Animals Conference (*www. takingactionforanimals.com*) in Washington, D.C.

DON'T ROLL OVER

If you're looking to agitate for change, but don't know where to begin, visit animal welfare activist websites such as the Humane Society (*www.hsus.org*), the ASPCA (*www.aspca.org*), PETA (*www.peta.org*), International Fund for Animal Welfare (*www.ifaw.org*), In Defense of Animals (*www.idausa.org*), and Last Chance for Animals (*www.lcanimal.org*). Discover their missions and key issues, and sign up for action alerts or to receive newsletters. This will clue you into animal welfare campaigns, boycotts, hearings for legislation, and demonstrations, as well as give you concrete direction for contacting political officials and signing petitions.

Don't underestimate the power of one.
When Chris Crawford adopted a German shepherd from a shelter, it was her first introduction to the difficulty Sheps and other big dogs have in finding a second home. The Virginia resident now describes herself as a shepherd activist. She talks the ears off anyone willing to listen about how fantastic her rescued dog is and the seriousness of six million dogs passing through shelters every year. Chris also created a video called *Rescue Me* to raise awareness about surrendered German shepherds. She distributes the video via YouTube, and some shelters and rescues use the DVD version.

If there's not an answer out there, find one.
Maybe the problem you want to solve doesn't have an organization with an answer. In 2003, Julie and Jim Dugan started the Dugan Foundation, a grassroots effort to end, within ten years, the practice of euthanasia as a form of pet-population control in their home community, Pierce County, Washington. At the time, there was minimal local support for a no-kill effort. The largest shelter, the Humane Society for Tacoma and Pierce County (with around 25,000 animals a year, the highest reporting agency in the state), openly stated "no-kill" was not possible.

So the Dugans mortgaged their home, called in favors, and threw a black-and-white fund-raiser called the Fur Ball. To everyone's surprise, they grossed $100,000. Since then, they have expanded their community efforts with projects including designing and building a high-volume spay-neuter facility; implementing a free, mobile spay-neuter program for low-income pet owners, adding a gratis day for free-roaming cats; and assisting a network of no-kill shelters with financial aid and business expertise. What's more, the local Humane Society now embraces the no-kill effort and is working toward a shelter solution by 2008.

Ask yourself: What do I bring to the cause?

You don't have to be an animal expert or a philanthropist. Jim and Julie Dugan are not veterinarians or handlers, nor are they a big-money family looking for a cause. They are ex-Starbucks corporate types with loads of project management savvy and development, construction design, and real estate experience. They realized these qualities could be an asset to other animal welfare organizations, which are often run on heart and a shoestring.

For example, while Jim was a volunteer at the Humane Society, he discovered that the bathing facilities at the shelter made it difficult to wash large dogs. Because the ungroomed pups were much less likely to be adopted, he instituted something called "Big Dog Wednesdays," when volunteers strong enough to lift big dogs into the elevated tubs came in for a bathing brigade. After the Dugan Foundation's first Fur Ball, they used the proceeds to design and build a larger washing facility at the shelter, with ramps that would accommodate large dogs. Because of their construction smarts and connections, they were able to do the job quickly and cost effectively.

Find out who's doing things right.

Don't reinvent something that has already been figured out. That's a lesson from the corporate world that the Dugans brought into their nonprofit venture. For example, they are modeling their high-volume spay and neuter clinic on plans created by the Humane Alliance in North Carolina. "You just make sure you don't go uphill when you don't need to," Julie says. "Most of the people in animal welfare now are so about solving problems, they hand you the plans."

Don't make your first meeting a poop party. Matt Van Wormer was galvanized into action after he was ticketed for playing Frisbee with his off-leash dog, Axel, in a Boulder park. Before that, he'd never really given any thought to leash laws in his town or politics. Within a year he was running meetings, making presentations to government officials, and heading up Friends Interested in Dogs and Open Space (FIDOS), a political group with major clout. Early on, he learned an important lesson. With an eye toward bringing together like-minded dog folk and scoring points with the Boulder parks, he invited people to clean up a regular park before meeting. "Well, you can imagine. Nobody wanted to come down and do poop pickup with me," he says. "That wasn't on anybody's agenda."

DREAM JOB: DOGA INSTRUCTOR

One of the more unusual places dogs and people come together these days is at the yoga studio. It's actually about time, when you consider that one of the basic poses, Downward Facing Dog, is more than a passing nod to stretching pups everywhere. Still, Doga, as it's sometimes called, is a bit of a detour off the standard K-9 highway.

For a long time, Seattle yoga instructor Brenda Bryan shooed her dogs Honey (a shar-pei–boxer) and Gus (a papillon–terrier) off the mat when she practiced at home. But when the local Humane Society asked her to create a yoga class with dogs, she immediately saw the logic of the thing and eagerly invited the dogs back.

"Dogs are pack animals, so I think they make natural yoga partners," Brenda says. Dogs participate in the practice in their own way. They sit or lie down (if you're lucky) and are incorporated into human poses, used to guide alignment, or as gentle supports. Sometimes Brenda gently stretches Gus's or Honey's legs or massages their ears, jaws, necks, chests, backs, and legs, and a dreamy look comes into their eyes.

It's not like a humans-only class. Usually there's a barker and a rambler. "It takes them a little while to adjust to being on the yoga mat," says Brenda, who, with Debra Harry–blonde hair and tattoos of Ganesh and the Chinese character for love on her biceps, is the picture of yogic health and style. "But the practice has a calming effect on the dog."

Brenda says dogs, like us, derive health benefits from massage, such as relaxation, tension relief, and improved circulation. Human participants get to know a dog's range of motion and become more familiar with their dog's bodies, which might help them to recognize if something is wrong.

Brenda believes that a true yogi would understand the presence of pups. "I use the class with the intention of bringing a deeper connection between people and their dogs," Brenda says, "and taking that feeling of connection out into the world."

Change thinking.

Matt also learned it's not enough to win small battles. "When you're dealing with city employees, you really have to get them on your side," he says. "If they're not, you may win for two or three years, but when you wear out, those people are going to slide their agenda right back in on you."

CANINE CAREERS

"In my previous job as an engineer, we'd go to all these meetings and all this other stuff. And when you get home, you say, 'Well, what did I accomplish today? Not a lot,'" says Jose Pico, a dog caregiver at Best Friends Animal Society in Utah. "But working with the dogs, every day when you get home, you are tired. You collapse in bed and you say, 'Oh, I had a good day. I did something constructive today.' It puts life in perspective."

Jose spends his days feeding and cleaning up after the dogs, administering medications, and walking residents, including those wearing "red collars" (who are too challenging for volunteers). After work, he fosters Xena, a flop-eared, black terrier mix with special needs who was found as a stray in 2006. It's a far cry from his life as an engineer in Orlando, Florida. His world changed with a one-week volunteering vacation at Best Friends in 2001, which turned into one week a year for five years. Eventually, he moved full-time to the land of red-rock canyons to work with puppies in need.

Every day, people are inspired to abandon day jobs or take second jobs to pursue a career that satisfies their dog-loving souls. Usually, a particular dog is to blame or praise for this dramatic action. But most of the people who've been able to make a go of it report that working in the furry trenches is a vast improvement over previous jobs.

Many of these efforts are entrepreneurial. As you may have noticed, I spotlight several dog-centric entrepreneurs—dog photographer, Doga instructor, dog fur-spinner, and more—as a window into how they do it and why. If there are any smarts to add here, it's a simple suggestion that you look before you leap.

Just because you're crazy about dogs doesn't mean you'll like or be good at working with them. It really takes a few nitty-gritty experiences to know if you can hang with it. Jamie Pflughoeft, a dog photographer and pet portrait artist in Seattle, broke into the dog biz as a professional walker. In the first hour of her first day as a walker-in-training, she arrived at the home of a pair of greyhounds with diarrhea. "I was on my hands and knees cleaning up," she remembers. "The smell made me want to vomit." But that experience, which still stands as her worst day on the job, didn't stop her. Later, she was bitten and dragged into mud—not everyone's cup of chai—but she walked dogs happily for five years and launched her photography business with many of the shots she took on that job.

Test-drive your dream.

While some folks just jump in, the best recommendation is baby steps. Create a do-it-yourself mentorship or internship with a professional in the line you'd like to try. If you're willing to help out for free, they might be willing to share their knowledge. Another option is to sign up for a Vocation Vacations' experience (*www.vocationvacations.com*). This Oregon business offers mentorships with an animal therapist, trainer, dog walker, day-care owner, kennel owner, or veterinarian—a way to glean valuable real-world experience before mortgaging the farm.

On the Trail

ASK PEOPLE WHY THEY HIKE WITH THEIR DOGS, and you'll get a variety of answers not all that different from the reasons we share our lives with them.

Shadow became Jim Greenway's hiking buddy when his two-legged friends no longer had time, conditioning, or inclination to join him. Amanda Tikkanen backpacks with Beau because the Louisiana catahoula leopard dog needs a job. Justin Lichter brings Yoni on thousand-mile treks because that's what he's doing and she's his dog.

Hiking with a dog can be a sublime experience. Watching my dog lope down the trail, sniffing big drams of marmot scent and piqued by the sound of twigs snapping, I begin to appreciate the wild universe in new ways. She is a window into another dimension, and she adds excitement and awe to the experience of a walk through the woods.

The pleasures are not strictly limited to the trail either. "You can't truly 'talk' to your dog about the trip when it's done," Jim Greenway says, "but there is an extra bond or energy in the relationship when, every time you scratch the dog's head, it prompts your recollection of all the great hikes you've had together. Those memories add extra value to the relaxation that most dog owners enjoy in interacting with their pets."

Hiking and camping with canines is a big bailiwick—the stuff of books. So this chapter makes no claims to comprehensiveness. Most of the wisdom here comes from topics hikers with dogs express the most interest in. It is focused on day hiking and backcountry camping, as opposed to car camping. (Much of the wisdom in the "On the Road" chapter applies to that front.)

I also don't talk much about the strategies and gear required for the human side of camping, except where it bears directly on your dog. But there is a crucial point on that score to be made: First and foremost, you need to be prepared for all your needs and exigencies. If anything happens to you—anything bad, that is—it's not good for the dog who depends on you. Keep yourself safe, happy, warm, well-nourished, and hydrated, and you'll be able to look after your charge, who, by the way, has no choice in the matter.

In the backcountry, the stakes are raised. You're usually a few hours, at least, from immediate help, subject to weather changes and wild animals, with only the supplies you and your dog are able to carry. (Why do we do this?) It's with that context in mind that many of the hikers in this chapter offer their trail-vetted wisdom.

HAPPY TRAILS, WAGGING TAILS

While dogs love wild areas, wild areas don't always love dogs. The National Park Service bans dogs on many trails, even leashed, although they do allow dogs in certain campgrounds (leashed) and in cars. Same for national monuments. National, state, and local wildernesses, parks, forests, recreation areas, and preserves each have their own rules, which are usually posted at trailheads and entrances. Here's the key: Never assume your dog is welcome. This will save you big disappointment after a long drive.

That said, there's no reason to despair. There are plenty of red-rock gulches, wildflower meadows, and snowy forests through which to trek. Room for everyone. But you'll have to do your research.

Consider this: There are usually lovely—and less crowded—dog-friendly alternatives near the marquee nature stops. Sure, dogs are not welcome at Baxter State Park (home of noble Mount Katahdin) in Maine, but they can glory in rocky trails and ocean breezes at Acadia National Park on Maine's coast. They can't crisscross the glaciers on Mount Rainier, but they can enjoy views of the majestic knob while trotting in the William O. Douglas Wilderness nearby. While Arches National Park in Utah is a canine no-go zone, you can find breathtaking rock formations on the dog-friendly Corona Arch Trail not far away. See the trick?

Learn about dog-friendly trails and areas from a variety of sources, including books dedicated to the subject. In unfamiliar areas, keep in mind regulations change, so hedge your bets and contact the managing agency for the latest facts. If you're staying at a dog-friendly B&B, ask the owners about nearby hiking. Check with hiking groups, dog stores, and outfitters near where you plan to hike. Online resources include many places to learn more, from everyday trailblazing bloggers to forums such as Traildog (see below).

Online Haven for Trail Dogs

Anyone who has posted a question about hiking with a dog to a general online hiking forum knows the responses aren't always hospitable. The topic of dogs on hiking trails evokes strong opinions. "Pose a question about trail dogs on, say, one of the Appalachian Trail email forums, and you're likely to have your whiskers singed," says Jim Greenway, the list owner for the Traildog group (*www.groups.yahoo.com/group/Traildog*).

When the north Georgia resident took over Traildog (which was formerly known as Dog-Hike), he used what he calls the "neighborhood bar" approach. "Traildog is a place where anyone who hikes with a dog can come in, relax, ask questions, share trip reports, and generally talk 'trail dogs.'" Back in the early days (mid-1990s), Greenway and other subscribers monitored general hiking lists for posts by new subscribers who didn't realize the consequences of asking about hiking with dogs. "Once those lists's other readers had 'flamed' the unfortunate subscriber to a crisp, one of us would privately email the freshly burned poster that he or she was welcome to post the question at Dog-Hike."

The approach succeeded. Traildog is probably the largest online dog-hiking list, with approximately 1,300 subscribers and a few hundred messages each month. Routine questions include everything from the ideal breed for hiking, where to hike, and dog regulations to dealing with first-aid emergencies, dog waste, and trail food. It's an excellent source of wisdom and camaraderie.

When Alan Bauer, of Fall City, Washington, is out hiking with his dog, Mittens (on-leash), he sees more wildlife, including elk, deer, grouse, and wild turkeys, than when he's alone. By himself, he'll walk right by and never know an animal is there. "Mittens doesn't bark. She'll freeze and I look up and there is a great horned owl in a tree," Alan says. "Or a bear in a valley 2,000 feet below."

BACKWOODS RULES

Not everyone will be happy to see you and your dog on the trail. Our four-footed friends have a reputation—more myth than reality—for bothering hikers, disturbing wildlife, and leaving waste behind, all problems that are the province of their people. Like so many aspects of the dog life, it's usually a few bad apples spoiling the experience for responsible hikers.

Here are a few of the standard practices—according to the good apples out there—for keeping wild places open to dogs.

On the Trail

- Hike with your dog on-leash or in voice control (depending on regulations). By the way, voice control means your dog will heel immediately on command and not bark, even when other hikers or tempting critters are nearby.
- If you're walking with your dog off-leash, keep her in your sightline and in voice control. You can't control your dog if you can't see her.
- Move off the trail with your dog when you see other hikers. Don't let your dog wiggle in for sniffs unless the other hikers ask to visit.
- Move well clear of the trail when you see mountain bikers, horses, or pack animals. It's best to wait on the downhill side of horses.
- Don't let your dog harass wildlife.

Waste management: Tying poop-filled plastic bags to the side of your dog's pack is a bad idea; the bags will puncture and tear on branches and brush.

THE ULTIMATE TRAIL DOG

In the contemporary annals of hiking dogs, it's hard to imagine a dog to compete with Yoni. With her trail buddy, Justin Lichter, the St. Bernard–Border collie mix has logged 20,000 trail miles, covering 10,000 in one year alone.

Yoni, who was born on an Idaho farm, looks like a sleek Swiss rescue dog, with only one of the characteristic brown eye patches. When Justin got her from a friend, he planned on hiking the Appalachian Trail with her the following year, but he had no clue that trek would be only the beginning.

On their first hike from Georgia to Quebec he took things slowly, learning the ins and outs of long-distance hiking at the same time he learned about hiking with a dog. By the time he set out on the Pacific Crest Trail (PCT), he was confident in his trail buddy, with whom he regularly walks more than thirty miles a day. The PCT hike took them from Mexico to Canada, with an additional detour from the Canadian border to Cape Alava on the Washington coast.

A year later, the duo hiked from Mexico to northern Alberta on the Continental Divide and Great Divide trails. Next up, Justin and Yoni trekked from Cape Gaspe to Key West on the International Appalachian and Appalachian trails, the Benton Mackaye Trail, the Georgia and Alabama Pinhote Trail, and the Florida Trail; then from Mexico to Canada on the Pacific Crest Trail; and finally from Canada to Mexico on the Continental Divide Trail.

"I think that what we do is not inherently in a dog's nature, since they usually seem to run and then rest, not walk steadily for long periods," Justin says. "It's incredible that she has picked up on so many tricks to adapt to it."

Yoni wears a backpack in which she carries a collapsible bowl, sometimes vitamins and dog treats, and high-calorie puppy food—two pounds per day, which Justin spikes with cooking oil. He doesn't carry any of her gear unless the stretch is more than five days without resupply. In that case, the dog food would be too heavy for her.

In all of these miles, she has never been seriously hurt, although one hot day in the Florida Keys, Justin treated her to a break from road walking by pushing her in a shopping cart. She did have a problem with a foxtail, which had to be removed by a vet, and another time she developed a limp, which was cured with four days' rest.

Sometimes Yoni leads. Other times, she walks in Justin's shadow. The few times she's been out of sight, she has come right back. "She is probably worried, since we walk so much and stay in different places every night, that if she loses me she may not find me," he says.

When they are on the trail together, Justin doesn't have to talk to Yoni much. "I think that we both just kind of know what each other is thinking," he says. "It is just like spending a lot of time with a person because there are times that I will get frustrated with her for something, maybe pulling a little bit on the leash or knocking over her food bowl. I also know that when I do get frustrated it is because I am starting to get a little bit dehydrated."

Justin is understated about his epic treks with Yoni. "I do these hikes because I like being outside and seeing things change with the seasons and living simply," he says. "I bring Yoni because she likes it."

Dogs can be an advantage for keeping varmints away from campsites. When mice in an Appalachian Trail shelter chewed a hole in Justin Lichter's backpack, he just stationed his hiking dog, Yoni, next to it and had no more problems.

In Camp

- If you're sharing a tent, backcountry hut, or trail shelter with others, be sure your dog is dry or leave him outside. Wet dogs aren't all that cozy.
- Begging, especially from drooling dogs, is another camping no-no.
- Dogs drink downstream from people.
- No digging. As at the dog park, holes on or near the campsite or trail are an eyesore and a potential hazard for other hikers and their dogs.

Wherever You Go

"Leave no trace" is a critical ethic for all campers. It's the simple principle of leaving the wilderness as you found it.

Day hikers should get in the habit of packing out dog waste. Seattleite Vikki Kauffman dedicates one dog pack for carrying out waste from her four poodles on day hikes and cross-country skiing outings.

In the backcountry, the rules for burying your own waste apply equally to your dog's (a 6- to 8-inch-deep hole more than 200 feet from water, campsites, and the trail). On a recent wilderness river trip with her dog, Ranger, Iowan Nora Boyd brought along a Scat Packer, one of several portable toilet systems for human refuse. She collected her retriever's poop and hauled it out with the human waste. Now that's motivated.

TRAIL PREP 101

Even if your dog looks like a wolf, years—not to mention, generations—of domestic bliss and couch surfing makes him ill-suited for extended pastoral wandering without a little physical and mental tuning.

Conditioning

We sometimes think of dogs as bionic—creatures who can leap off the bed after hibernating all winter and tackle long treks. But veterans know out-of-shape quadrupeds get cramps, develop sore muscles, and even become exhausted without proper conditioning. Trail savvy guardians build up to serious hiking. In addition to walks (with and without a pack), try cross-training with your dogs by running, playing retrieving games and hide-and-seek, and on warm days, swimming, which keeps them cool and builds strength.

Altitude is another issue. Carolyn Eddy, who keeps pack goats at sea level in Portland, Oregon, attends an annual pack-goat rendezvous in the Rocky Mountains at altitudes around 10,000 feet. She prepares by hiking with her Border collie, Bob, on Mount Hood, about an hour from home, along trails at 5,000 to 6,000 feet. In addition, she, Bob, and the goats acclimate to the Rockies gradually during a four-day drive to the trailhead.

When she is hiking at altitude, Carolyn watches Bob's hydration as closely as her own. He and the goats drink half-strength Gatorade for the electrolytes—just like people. She also suggests making sure your dog eats, even if it means giving him or her "people food," because altitude can take the edge off an otherwise healthy dog's appetite. When it comes to his food, Bob's luckier than most trail dogs. Carolyn's goats haul his chow.

Training

Train your trail pooch not to chase wildlife. Some hikers practice this in a yard or park with birds and squirrels. When their dog spies a bushy brown tail, a flickering feather, or the whiskers of a neighbor's cat, they tell him or her to sit or stay and provide rewards for the proper restraint. This is just as important for on-leash dogs as free-ranging ones. There are plenty of moments on the trail—log bridges or narrow ledges—where a dog suddenly pulling on a leash can be treacherous. Maintaining balance with a heavy pack is hard enough without a dog jerking the leash.

Train your dog to wait, sit, or stay at water sources, even when thirsty. This protects him from slurping up algae-thick or cowpie-riddled ponds. It's also important for keeping dogs out of streams where fellow (potentially non-dog-loving) humans are collecting water.

Train them to stay close. Trekkers who let their dogs off-leash teach their dogs to keep track of them with games of hide and seek. The ideal is to have a dog who wants to know where his person is at all times.

GEAR UP

It's easy to envy dogs. They are so self-contained, with all-purpose coats and versatile paws. They get by on food, water, and just a few accouterments. But on the trail, they do require some extras to keep them safe and happy.

Leashes

Long-distance hiker Justin Lichter covers the miles with Yoni on-leash, which he attaches to her collar when she is walking behind (on warm days) or the ring on the back of her dog pack when she's out in front. Nature photographer Alan Bauer prefers a flexible leash for Mittens—not the extension type but the Bungee cord style (sometimes called absorber leads), which he clips to his backpack. This leaves his hands free to, among other things, take photos.

Vikki Kauffman uses her skijoring harness when she hikes with her poodles in the summer. "It's great for backpacking because they pull you up hill, it makes it so much easier," she says. Plus, a harness also leaves your hands free. You can buy skijoring and running harnesses, or adapt climbing harnesses for this purpose. Vikki made her own with flat webbing and a quick-release carabiner.

In the winter, she also puts bells on her poodles' collars to alert other skiers to their presence. For Haley Poulos in Silverdale, Washington, dog tags are multipurpose when she hikes in the Cascade Mountains with her dog, Charlotte. "I keep Char's collar on her at all times," Haley says. "The jingle on her collar has alerted more than one bear that we were in the area."

If you hike with your dog off-leash, keep his or her recall skills sharp by frequently practicing at home and on the trail.

Brian Bate in Portland, Oregon, keeps a whistle attached to his pack with which he calls Hank, his German shepherd–rotweiler mix. Brian has two different whistle patterns. One means "Come here," the other "Don't go any farther." The whistle carries well over the noise of river and distances.

Dog Packs

It's a truth universally acknowledged that getting your dog to wear a pack is a good thing. A pack helps share the burden, gives dogs a sense of purpose, and tends to make them less intimidating to strangers. But not all packs are created equal and finding the right one can take patience and persistence.

Don't play the heavy.

Most hikers recommend your dog carry between 10 to 20 percent of his body weight, and that most of the weight rest up near the dog's shoulders. Be sure not to add all the weight at once. Break your dog into the pack and add weight slowly with fun walks and lots of praise.

Do your research.

There are two central bugaboos when it comes to dog packs—improper fit and inadequate training. Because dogs vary in size, shape, length, fur type, strength, and so on, there's no way to recommend a one-pack-for-all solution. There are also economic considerations. Read the opinions of uncompensated hikers who field test gear, including dog packs, and then post their evaluations at the website *www.backpackgeartest.org.*

Traildog member Amanda Tikkanen is one such reviewer,

Saddlebags must be evenly weighted. Water bottles are a good way to fine-tune balance. Kibble in several separate bags also works pretty well.

Balance saddlebags by putting the same thing in each. Some Portland, Oregon, winemakers I know carry their dog's food when they trek into their ski-in cabin, while she carries two bottles of wine in her pack, one on each side.

but she also shakes down dog and people gear at her eclectic website Uberpest's Journal (*www.uberpest.com*). Even better, Amanda provides plenty of how-to's, FAQs, and recycle-minded, budget-conscious instructions for how to make everything from dog boots to harnesses. Fresh out of high school, she converted an old saddlebag into a dog pack for her first trail buddy, Lucy, a Catahoula leopard–Australian cattle dog mix. Her personal blog follows her adventures with Beau, another catahoula leopard dog, in the ring and on the trail, and is loaded with common-sense advice.

Prevent buckle failure.
In all his years backpacking with dogs and selling dog packs on eBay, North Carolina–based hiker Mark Ball has seen only two consistent causes of pack failure—broken buckles (usually after being stepped on in the dark) and holes chewed by scavenging mice, a hungry dog, or even a bear. He recommends carrying zip ties in case a buckle fails. But prevention is the best strategy. Hang your dog's pack in a campsite or picnic spot to prevent clumsy feet or marauders from doing damage. Even if you're not spending the night, it only takes a squirrel a half hour to wreak havoc while you splash around in a lake.

Booties
Snowballs in pads. Thorns. Sharp lava. Simple trail wear and tear. There are plenty of reasons for a dog to wear booties (including the funny dance they do when you first put them on). Even if your dog doesn't dig them, you want boots in reserve

Bright colors and reflective tape aren't essential but they can help keep dogs safe when hunters are about. On day hikes, high-visibility vests are a good idea.

Remember to regularly check booties for fit—they'll stretch with use and when they get wet.

Nora Boyd packs infant socks. If her Pembroke corgi, Gryphon, hurts one of his pads, she's found the little sock fixed with tape is the easiest way to dress it.

Other options for securing dogs at a campsite are crates or collapsible exercise pens—though obviously more appropriate for car camping.

Some campers prefer a dirty tent to letting dogs sleep outside, where they can get into trouble if they tangle in a tie-out or, worse, tangle with wildlife.

in case he or she cuts a pad. I've seen a sixty-pound Lab mix carried miles to a trailhead—because his pads were shot.

Other paw tricks: Paw wax products are excellent for protecting paws on rocky or gravelly trails. Some hikers fortify their dog's paws by spraying Pad-Tough on the pads for a few weeks before a long-distance hike. Others follow the lead of mushers, giving dogs zinc supplements before an extended trek. Also, remember to trim nails before hikes.

Seattle skijorer Vikki Kauffman clips the fur on her poodles' paws before they head into snow. A typical practice for sled dogs, this helps prevent snowballs from forming. She sprays the cooking-oil spray PAM on their pads for the same purpose.

Tie-outs

Lots of campers and hikers suggest bringing tie-outs (a stake and cables) to secure dogs, especially at campsites where the aroma of open-fire smoked grub lures many a disciplined dog from home base. Melanie B., who lives on a farm with eight cats and six dogs in Alberta, Canada, has used tie-outs camping or temporarily on the farm. It helps her manage two roaming Great Pyrenees—Hank and Baba—who don't like to come when they are called.

She strongly recommends that harnesses be used, so if the dog starts running like crazy he won't choke when he reaches the end of the rope. She also uses a maximum of twenty feet in length. She prefers coated wire because it's easier to clean and sturdier than rope. She won't use a chain, because she once had a dog catch a claw in one.

Tents

From the stories I hear, it appears that efforts to keep dirty, sometimes wet dogs outside tents are hopeless. So campers have devised several strategies—including these three—for keeping sleeping bags clean and dry:

1. *Towels.* When camping with her golden retriever, Holly, Carol Beebee carries two dog towels. The "paw towel" does the heavy-duty dog wipe down and gets really dirty. (Holly knows to sit and offer a paw for the "do paws" command, which makes life easy.) The other towel is for Holly to sleep on in the tent. "It's supposed to protect the sleeping bags," the former travel nurse says. "Although it doesn't always work that way."
2. *Timing.* Set up your dog's bed before you lay out your own sleeping bag. Even if your dog normally hops right up when you need her to move, it might be more of a challenge to get her off a comfy sleeping bag when she's tired from a long day of hiking.

3. *Elevation*. One way to keep muddy, wet, dirty, stinky dogs off your sleeping bag is to elevate it. Sleeping in a hammock under a tarp keeps your sleeping bag clean and keeps you away from the cold, hard ground. Tie your dog to the hammock tree, at the same end as your head, so you can check on her and she can check on you. Throw a little pad under the tent or hammock to protect her hardworking joints and keep her dry.

Car campers can use crates in the vestibule to keep pups close by, but not too close.

Other Hiking Tackle
Sunscreen, string cheese, and duct tape are just a few of the items you'll find in the stuff sacks of hikers with canine buddies.

No need to go all Survivor all the time.
Why leave all the comforts of home behind? When Haley Poulos packs for her dog, Charlotte, she brings a couple comfort items, including a favorite Frisbee and a Kong (and something to stuff it with), to keep Charlotte busy while they're sitting around a campfire. "I think it's a good idea to bring a familiar blanket from home for some pups, especially if they've never slept in a tent before," Haley says.

Remember duct tape.
No book about grassroots wisdom would be complete without a tip of the baseball cap to duct tape. North Carolina hiker Mark Ball wraps two to three feet of duct tape around a tent stake.

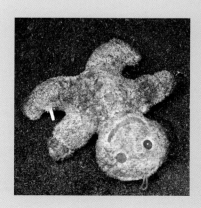

Take a class: In an actual emergency, as they say, flipping through a book or reviewing a quick-reference chart can waste valuable time. If you plan to hike frequently or far from civilization, why not take a pet first-aid class? Certain chapters of the American Red Cross and other organizations offer instruction in everything from pet CPR to shock management.

After an especially steep or difficult trail, consider giving your dog one-half to one buffered aspirin (ask your vet about dosage). Like the rest of us, dogs' joints stiffen after a rigorous hike and the aspirin helps. It worked for Denali, my editor Kate Rogers's husky mix. Kate also recommends glucosamine tablets or chews for long-term joint care.

(For day hikers, water bottles or walking sticks are keen surfaces for storing the waterproof tape.) It takes up no extra space and helps in a pinch. Mark has used duct tape on a cut finger and a torn backpack. It was also called into service when, for the first time in five years, he left his first-aid kit behind and his dog tore a pad. "I used one of my socks and a piece of duct tape to make a boot that lasted the rest of the trip," Mark says.

Carry pocket posters.

On the trail, Brian Bate carries about a half-dozen wallet-size pictures of his dog, Hank, with contact information printed on waterproof paper. "If he were to take off on the trail and we weren't able to find him," Brian says, "I could pass these out to hikers on the trail rather than having to go all the way back home and make a poster and suddenly he's 300 miles away." As a manager at a Portland, Oregon, REI, Brian shares this suggestion with customers who hike with dogs.

Pack a first-aid kit.

Be prepared for canine and human emergencies on the trail. The farther you are from the trailhead, the more independent you'll need to be. Make a few pet-specific additions to your regular first-aid kit, including an animal emergency quick-reference guide, a muzzle (for an upset puppy), an oral-dosing syringe, canine hydrocortisone ointment, Benadryl, buffered aspirin, hydrogen peroxide, tea-tree oil for cuts, vet wrap, tweezers for thorns, and canine sunscreen for thin-coated pups (especially around the ears and nose).

TRAIL GRUB

For day hiking, water is by far the most important item for dogs. Most hikers let their dogs drink from decent-looking water sources, although there can be concerns about microscopic parasites such as *Giardia*. But be prepared to carry, or have your dog carry, water. One of you might also carry a water filter and/or purification tablets.

One advantage to packing water for your dog or purifying river water is that it reduces the amount your dog has to scavenge along the edge of fragile lakes and rivers. It also cuts down on how wet and muddy your dog might be when it's time to crawl into the tent.

Intrepid traveler Carol Beebee discovered that having a designated dog-only (wide-mouth) bottle or two is a big help, especially when water is at a premium. This way if a dog doesn't finish what you pour into her collapsible bowl, you can pour it back into the dog bottle. No water is lost. Carol always keeps a full dog bottle in the fridge (everyone knows it's Holly's) so the water is cold and ready for her adventures.

MOUNTAIN BIKING WITH A CANINE CO-PILOT

Dogs are becoming a more frequent sight on mountain-bike trails, and it can be a blast to have them along. Mark Peterson has been riding with his golden retriever, Kaya, for nine years. She's a perfect companion, setting the pace up hill and then trotting close behind on the descent. To the untrained eye, man and dog come awfully close to colliding at times.

Despite appearances, collisions are the least of a rider's challenges when it comes to mountain biking with dogs. A trail veteran and president of Whatcom Independent Mountain Pedalers in Bellingham, Washington, Mark worries that not all cyclists understand the unique issues of riding with a dog.

"People forget that bikes are super efficient," he says. "You can't just go out and get exercise for yourself because that's not really fair to the dog." They are working far harder per mile, with far less efficient cooling systems.

"The trick of riding with a dog is to always be aware of them. I've ridden with Kaya long enough that I know where she's at," Mark says. Normally, she's champing to get ahead and barking at Mark if he stops. That's how he knows she has plenty of fuel left. "When she's tired, she'll drop back behind me and pretty much run the same pace I ride. If I notice she's getting tired, I'll drop my pace until she's in front again."

Dogs push themselves to their limit and won't slow down until they are done. Mark has seen the consequences of ignoring a few simple dog-smart guidelines firsthand. He helped a rider evacuate an exhausted chocolate Lab in a wheelbarrow but was too late to save him.

Mark's tips for dog-safe mountain biking include these:

- Leave your dog at home on warm days.
- Let your dog set the pace.
- Work up to longer rides. Dogs, like people, need conditioning.
- Know your dog's strengths and weaknesses. Not all breeds are built for high-intensity endurance workouts.
- Do not allow your dog to eat or drink large amounts before vigorous exercise.
- Keep your dog hydrated, just like yourself, with small quantities of water at frequent intervals. Mark carries a collapsible nylon bowl that he can fill out of his hydration pack, and he brings an extra bottle in the water cage on his bike.
- Be able to recognize signs of overexertion and heat exhaustion. If your dog is dragging way behind you, you are riding too fast. If your dog's head begins to drop below shoulder level, he's in the red zone. Stop immediately. Get him to shade and cool him down with your water or water from a stream. Walk out slowly with plenty of rest breaks. Get him to the vet.

Trail Treats

There are lots of treats formulated for hiking dogs. But Haley Poulos brings Charlotte's favorite peanut butter biscuits rather than risk upsetting her tummy with something new. Oily salmon treats are good, fatty energy food for hiking dogs. Jim Greenway limits salmon to hikes, which gives his dog an extra reason to want to hit the trail. Vikki Kaufman brings hard-boiled eggs.

Even if you stick to the same brand when mixing types of dog food, consider transitioning your dog from the "maintenance" diet to the "hiking" diet *before* the trip to avoid stomach upset.

Dog Park Wisdom photographer Bev Sparks likes to use string cheese as her on-the-road Kong stuffing. You can take the low-fat, prewrapped tubes anywhere, and one smushes perfectly inside a small Kong.

Beware Mr. Bear. Remember to put dog food, chewies, and bones in bear bags or boxes at night, especially if you decide to bring salmon along for your dog.

Food for Longer Trips

The first time I took Satchel (my Lab–shepherd mix) back-packing, she buried her kibble. For four meals in a row, she knocked over her floppy bowl and pushed loose dirt in with the food. I cleared it up and ended up packing out all of her kibble plus dirt. Thankfully, we had too much human food on that trip. She ended up eating salami, cheese, oranges, soup, and energy bars along with us.

Apparently she's not alone. Other traveling dogs act funny about their food on the road, burying or ignoring it. Jim Greenway's dog, Shadow, was prone to burying his food on the first couple of days of camping or business trips. Shadow would use his muzzle to try to cover the bowl with leaf litter when they were in the woods or brush his muzzle around the carpet, as if he were raking invisible dirt into his bowl, when they were in a hotel. Sometimes Jim, manager of the Traildog group on Yahoo.com, sprinkled garlic powder (not garlic salt) onto the food—an idea he picked up from musher/author Gary Paulsen. Other times, he used a canine food supplement called The Missing Link. Either option usually perked up Shadow's appetite.

After a one- to three-night camping trip, most people bring home more of their dog's food than they expected they would. It sometimes takes a dog's appetite a couple of days to kick in. Once it does, most dogs will eat just about anything. They're in no danger of starving, as they usually have plenty of fat to power them. Jim recommends sticking to a dog's regular diet unless he or she is on "weight-reducing" food. On longer trips, he has mixed about one-third of his dog's regular food with two-thirds of the same manufacturer's "high calorie" or "active dog" food. Keeping to the same brand permits you to increase the caloric intake with less risk of upsetting the dog's stomach.

Some campers bring along canned wet food to entice otherwise travel-picky eaters (a tip that works for anyone traveling with a dog, not just camping). On the trail, wet food can be heavy to pack in and messy to pack out. If you're really distraught about the thought that your dog won't eat, try taking along one of the foil-packed pouches of salmon. They're in the canned meats aisle near the tuna. Stir some salmon and salmon oil from the foil pack into the dog's food. You'll want a heavy-duty, reclosable plastic bag, too.

PESKY PESTS

Because they are low-to-the-ground, covered in fur, and have a tendency to stick their curious muzzles into dark corners, dogs can get into a whole lot of hurt on the trail. All sorts of natural pesky things are out there that you need to be ready for. Here's a partial list with some creative coping strategies.

Foxtails and Burrs

Burrs love to twist and tangle in dog fur. Brushing them out can be painful, for you and your dog. Sometimes cutting burrs out with nail scissors is the easiest fix. As a preventative measure, some people spray mink oil conditioner on a dog's fur, making it too slippery for burrs to grab hold.

Like a burr's evil twin is the foxtail. These arrowlike grass seeds—common in the South-west—can be bad news. Foxtails have tiny barbs along their surface. Once they are picked up by your dog's fur (usually around the paws, nose, or ears), movement causes the barbed arrow to burrow under the skin. The seed can travel through a dog's body with nasty consequences.

As a precaution, pack a small, plastic, fine-toothed flea comb to help remove foxtails, burrs, and other grass seeds from dogs' coats after they walk in grassy areas.

Poisonous plants are another argument for keeping your dog on the cleared trail.

Justin Lichter's über hiker, Yoni, stepped on a foxtail, unbeknownst to both of them, somewhere in Southern California. About a week or so later, he noticed an oozing cut opened on her leg about three inches above her paw. He thought she had cut herself and treated it with Neosporin. They continued to hike thirty-plus miles per day and she didn't have any issues. A couple weeks later, though, the cut was still open. He left the trail and took her to a vet, who pulled a foxtail out of the cut. Two days later, it had healed over and that was that.

Poison Ivy, Oak, and Sumac

It's a good idea to know if poison ivy, oak, or sumac is growing along the trail and to be able to identify the plants; but even if you're plant smart and wearing pants, you can get into trouble.

These three leafy witches of the apocalypse produce a resin called urushiol, which causes an allergic reaction, a rash, irritation, and itching. Generally, if dogs come into contact with these plants, their fur protects them. But if you pet your dog after she just brushed against a poison oak plant, the oil can be transferred from her fur to your skin just as if you brushed the plant yourself. Carry an anti-itch cream containing cortisone in your first-aid kit. For you, not your dog.

The only way to remove urushiol is by washing your dog with soap and water—but this can also bring you into contact with the oil. If you can give your dog a bath, wear gloves, safety glasses, and long sleeves and pants to avoid a spray of itchy residue when your wet dog shakes.

Fleas, Flies, and Ticks

Chris Crawford finds that even her monthly topical tick repellent isn't enough to keep her German shepherd, Abby K9, tick-free in the Virginia woods, especially if it's nearly time for the next month's application. So she fortifies Abby's regular protection (in her case Frontline Top Spot) with a flea-and-tick collar when they're hiking or camping. "We've not seen a tick since, but carry a pair of special tick tweezers just in case," Chris says.

Chris uses either a traditional tick collar or she loops Bug-Bands wristband (for humans) around Abby's collar or pack. The active ingredient in BugBands is geraniol, extracted from geraniums, which makers say is safe to use around food and with pets.

Try this tick removal trick.
When Cloude Porteus walks his dogs, Lebowski and Linus, in tall grass in Northern California, the dogs get ticks—close to a couple dozen a year. Cloude's sister-in-law Kathy told him about an unusual technique for removing the pests, but he doubted her wisdom until he saw his vet do the same thing.

His old method was to clamp onto the tick close to where

the head was buried in poor Lebowski's or Linus's skin, usually near their eyes and ears, and pull straight out—often leaving the tick head behind and creating little scars. His new method is a lot flashier and effective. Here's how it's done:

- *Rub the tick in a circular motion.* Pretend you're trying to make it dizzy. Cloude generally sticks with one direction, clockwise, and rubs until the tick pulls out on its own. It usually takes less than a minute, so if it's not working, make sure the body of the tick is moving around. "I doubt the tick actually gets dizzy," he says, "but they sure don't like something about the movement."
- *Possible troubles.* When you catch the tick early in its attaching process, it makes it harder to actually get the body of the tick to move around. If it won't pull out, Cloude will usually wait another day instead of risking leaving part of the tick behind in his dog.
- *Tick disposal.* Once you have liberated the tick, flush it down the toilet. If they don't sink, they can crawl out. Other folks prefer to smother the liberated tick in alcohol or set it on fire. (Clearly, there some unresolved tick issues at work here.)

Cloude posted his tick-removal instructions, complete with a video, at *www.instructables .com* where he is a product manager. The feedback from Instructables's users who say they've followed his instructions is paws up.

Fur So Soft

There are dog-safe insect repellents (and sun screens) on the market, but Avon's Skin So Soft—the original formulation, not the spray—has devoted followers among dog folk as a flea, fly, and mosquito repellent.

When Joey had dozens of fleas and was too young for topical treatments or pills, Seattleite Taresa D. washed her in the sink with warm water and a capful of Avon's Skin So Soft. A relative had told Taresa about being issued Skin So Soft as an insect repellent in the Marines. After two washings, a combing out, and a couple of days, the fleas were gone. For her dog Tori, Taresa uses topical flea ointment but adds Skin So Soft when she needs a mosquito repellent. The triple-S is also put to work as a treatment for dry skin (diluted in water for bathing) and to remove tar or asphalt from pads.

Porcupines and Skunks

Hikers in porcupine country carry needle-nose pliers in case of a run-in. Even if you can't pull all the quills out, removing the ones from around your dog's nose, eyes, and throat before hiking out or driving to the vet can be a help.

Generally, you need a veterinarian's assistance to completely dequill your unhappy hound. Anne Henshaw has pulled countless quills out of her dogs in Petersburg, Alaska. But she is also an assistant for spay-neuter programs in Alaska and Mexico and a groomer, so she's not squeamish. She says it's a bloody, tricky business that usually requires sedation (for the dog, not the owner, who could probably use it too).

Since not all dogs learn from the experience, Anne has become a bit of a porcupine expert. She knows the little pincushions prefer alder stands to the open muskeg and deep woods near her Alaska home. Under cabins is another danger zone, since porcupines like to make their homes there. "If a dog is digging under a cabin in porcupine country, you want to leash it right now!" she says. If you're taking a multiday hike in porcupine country, the best policy is probably to keep your dog on a leash.

Stink No More

Tomato juice, a bottle of Sprite, or orange pulp and dish soap are among the many deskunking recommendations floating out there. But it took the brain of a non-dog-owning chemist to nail the fix. In the early 1990s, Paul Krebaum, a chemist in Illinois, was working on a reaction that produced hydrogen sulfide gas, which left a stinky waste stream. Much to the relief of co-workers, he concocted a mix of alkaline hydrogen peroxide to clear the air. When a colleague's cat got skunked, he remixed his recipe to neutralize the poor feline's odor. It worked. First published in *Chemical & Engineering News* in 1993, the skunk spray recipe spread among dog lovers by word of mouth and via the Internet. Today, it's the gold standard.

After a hard day on the trail and when the mosquitoes are bad, around dusk, let your dog hang out in the tent and snooze away unmolested. Just be sure to move your sleeping bag out of the way.

Deskunking Recipe
1 quart of 3 percent hydrogen peroxide
¼ cup baking soda
1 to 2 teaspoons liquid soap

In a plastic bucket, mix all ingredients. If you need more to cover a large dog, add one quart of tepid tap water.

Wash your pet thoroughly, working the solution deep into the fur. Let your nose guide you. Leave the solution on for about five minutes or until the odor is gone. Some heavily oiled areas may require a rinse and a repeat washing.

Skunks will usually spray a dog's face, so you'll need to wash there. But be sure to keep the solution out of your pet's eyes; it stings. If you have any cuts on your hands, you might want to wear latex gloves for the same reason. After treatment, thoroughly rinse your pet with tepid tap water.

Pour the spent solution down the drain with running water.

Never, ever store mixed solution in a closed bottle or sprayer. Pressure will build up until the container bursts. This can cause severe injury.

Use clean plastic mixing containers and utensils. Metals encourage decomposition of the peroxide. Remember, the quicker you treat your pet, the less work you'll have to do later. The peroxide mixture must come into contact with the skunk spray in order to neutralize it. As time passes, the skunk spray soaks deeper into the hair shaft and skin, making washing a more time-consuming process.

Snakes

If you live in rattlesnake country, find out if rattlesnake avoidance training is offered in your area. Nichole Royer puts her dogs through a program offered by Patrick Callaghan (*www. patrickcallaghan.com*) in which dogs are taught to recognize rattlesnakes by sight, sound, and scent, and to actively avoid being bitten.

She swears by it, with good reason. A few years back, she was out running a sled team of dogs. They were pulling her in a three-wheel cart on the dirt roads in the desert near her home in Lancaster, California. She was more than five miles from her car and cruising along at a nice steady trot.

Her team started up a steep hill and cranked into four-wheel-drive beautifully. Her malamute Kwest was running single lead, but as he crested the hill, he suddenly swung to the right and brought the entire team around and back down the hill. "It was as pretty a 'come gee' as I could have asked for except that I hadn't asked for it," Nichole says. "And in the process of doing it, the team yanked my cart sideways half-way up a steep hill and I almost ended up rolling the whole thing."

Adrenaline pumping, she had choice words to say to Kwest. "I was very much not pleased," she says. But nothing she yelled made any difference. At the bottom of the hill, she locked the brake down and turned the team by hand. The second she let go, Kwest turned back.

Finally, in complete frustration, she marched to the top of the hill to explain in great detail what she wanted. "I never made it that far," she says. "As I got to the top of the hill, I kicked a rock and up popped this little head together with that ominous *buzzzz* that just makes the hair on the back of my neck stand on end."

If her lead dog had topped the hill, the entire team would have overrun the sunbathing snake. Several dogs and Nichole could have been bitten. Getting the team home would have been a nightmare. "I went back down that hill, put my arms around Kwest's neck, and apologized in every way I could think of," she says. "I also thanked my lucky stars that he'd been through the rattlesnake avoidance clinic."

Nora Boyd also brings Dexamethasone in her first aid kit. She got a prescription from her vet (a vial and a small, disposable syringe). If Gryphon or Ranger has a run-in with a rattlesnake, Dex could help keep the dog from going into shock and give Nora the time she would need to get medical help.

On the Road

ROAD TRIPS WITH DOGS COME WITH CHALLENGES, such as fur in your fries, nose prints on the window, and extra pit stops. They also require more research upfront to find accommodations and attractions that welcome canine tourists. But the joys outweigh these small inconveniences. Chief among them is that with a canine copilot, you explore places you might otherwise miss.

It's not just the landscape that opens up under a pup's sniffer. People do, too. In his day, Jiggy Dawg, a compact white-and-brown pit bull terrier, was a terrific icebreaker. With big brown eyes, floppy ears, and a white stripe down his nose, he could coax a smile and conversation out of the most restrained local—even those whose jobs depended on keeping a skeptical distance.

Take the balmy night in Florida, a few weeks after 9/11, when Jiggy and his travel buddy, Ken Hoeve, napped near the Melbourne town water supply. "All of a sudden, there is a flashlight in my face and Jiggy is growling," Ken remembers. It was the cops on heightened alert.

Ken explained to the officers that he and his dog were in the middle of an 800-mile bicycle-and-kayak trek along Highway A1A and the Intercoastal Waterway to raise money for a summer camp for youth cancer patients. The cops appeared unimpressed until Jiggy jumped on the back of Ken's sport utility bicycle, demonstrating how he could balance on the skateboard-like platform over the back tire.

"They thought it was the coolest darn thing, once they figured out that I'm no terrorist," Ken says. The pair was allowed to stay and the police called around so fellow officers would give them the all clear. "It was because of Jiggy. He opened people's hearts up."

As dog-fueled road trips go, Ken's qualifies as epic. With not much more than a charity and a destination in mind, the duo peddle-paddled from Savannah to Key West. Ken hitched a fourteen-foot sea kayak to one side of his Xtracycle's back tire and a deflated raft to the other. The agile pup perched on top. Whenever they needed a change of scene, Ken would blow up the raft and tow it behind the kayak with the bicycle, gear, and Jiggy aboard.

Six years later, after a battle with cancer, Jiggy died at the Colorado ranch where he had retired from high-profile road trips. Even when Jiggy was sick, Ken never doubted his companion's memories of that journey. If he did, giving Jiggy a glimpse of the dismantled Xtracycle reassured him. "When I pulled that thing out, Jiggy was like, 'ruff, ruff, ruff, ruff,'" Ken says. "I could barely get the front tire on before he was on top of it, ready to go."

Ken's journey sets a pretty extreme bar for dog travel. Not surprisingly, the most common advice out there is not "pop your pup on the back of your bike for a nearly 1,000-mile ride." Even Ken nearly gave up on the first day of pedaling his fully loaded Xtracycle into the wind. But *Dog*

Park Wisdom tipsters agree on one thing: We owe our dogs adventures—afternoons at the lake, a day in the mountains, a weekend with dog-loving relatives, a week at dog camp, and on and on.

WHERE, OH WHERE, SHOULD MY LITTLE DOG GO?

Begin planning your trip with your dog's delight in mind. Ask yourself, has your Southern pup ever rolled in snow? Your landlubber ever felt a salty wave break across his chest? Your farm dog ever inhaled the bouquet of a fire hydrant in a major metropolis? Your foster hound ever snacked on carob bonbons in a four-star suite? Write up a list of all the things you want to do with your pup. Making your dog happy makes for a great baseline planning strategy, because when fur baby is happy, aren't we all?

That said, trying to jimmy a place for a dog (especially a big, furry, exuberant dog) on a people-centered trip isn't always a good idea. Long drives with few pit stop opportunities or long flights to not-so-dog-friendly cities aren't ideal. Barbara DeBry, a travel agent for people and their companion animals, usually urges her clients to leave the dog at home when it comes to business trips. You might want them nearby, she says, "but what is there for them to do while you're working?"

Beach

Despite movies like *Air Bud Spikes Back,* wherein the multitalented golden retriever kicks tail in beach volleyball, more and more waterfront, especially ocean beaches, is off limits to dogs. But there are workarounds.

Some beaches, especially in colder climates, permit dogs in the off-season. With a little research and a willingness to stroll under cloudy skies, dog people treat their buddies to beach-combing bonanzas.

Also, there are still some off-leash beaches (by law or by practice) out there. Call a dog boutique, a doggie day care, or a dog walker in your destination city or town to learn the real-world rules that aren't listed in books or on official websites. Dog people are nothing if not resourceful.

Coastal tipsters know salt water can cause vomiting and diarrhea. (Don't count on your swimming dog not to drink it because it tastes bad. Sometimes they can't help swallowing big mouthfuls.) Bring fresh water and be sure your dog takes beverage breaks. Rinsing or even washing a dog after swimming—and rolling in smelly kelp, rotting fish, and tidal debris—can help reduce the chances of skin irritations.

If you plan to hang out at the beach, bring an umbrella or a tarp and stakes for shade. Ask about jellyfish or other potentially nasty surprises in unfamiliar waters. Lots of aromatic waste washes up on the beach and some of it can be bad news for dogs. I heard of one dog who may have been fatally sickened from eating otter scat in Washington's San Juan Islands.

Remember, swimming in the ocean is more exhausting than in a lake. Watch out for overexertion or strong undertows. A life vest is a good idea even for a strong swimmer.

Wild Outdoors

There is nothing more divine than a quiet wood or a country stream or miles of trail for an outdoorsy human-dog duo. In fact, camping, hiking, snowshoeing, and the rest are so much the stuff of dog dreams, I've dedicated a whole chapter to them. Check out "On the Trail" for more al fresco wisdom.

Frozen water: Don't overlook snow trips. Not only can you avoid worries about overheating, most dogs go bananas in snow. I mean super-duper, prancing, skidding, rolling, nutso in snow. (It's like mud without the cleanup).

Canine pool parties: It's not always easy to find a canine-oriented swimming hole. In cities around the country, many community pools open for a dog swim before they are emptied for the season. Sometimes these puppy pool parties raise funds for good causes. Check with your community recreation department or local paper for details.

Ducks and marine animals at a safe distance from shore can motivate a dog to make the leap (see opposite page). My dog jumped off a friend's dock for the first time when she saw a river otter along the banks. Not something we planned, or even anticipated, but effective nonetheless.

Alert: The cousin of a friend was surprised when he showed up at a national hotel chain in Sioux Falls to discover his dog was not permitted. After driving from Chicago with his fuzzy buddy, he had to kennel him during the weekend-long family reunion. Although many hotel chains *are* pet-friendly, the policy can vary depending on local ownership. Be sure to double-check at your specific hotel.

Still, while we're on the subject of rustic pleasures, ever consider a fishing trip for Fido? I know it sounds weird. It's easy to imagine dogs causing a rumpus in the water and scaring fish away. But that's often not the case. Dogs can be as focused and patient as any human angler. Cheri McDonald discovered that her newly rescued Border collie was not the Frisbee dog she'd assumed but harbored watery ambitions.

Just two weeks after adding their first dog to the family, Cheri brought Rob Dog along on a river fly-fishing trip. The first day, on-leash, he sat on the bank and watched her fish. The next day, off-leash, he did the same. He's been that way ever since. Sometimes he wades in with Cheri and waits by her side. "He sees the fish under the water. If you don't cast, he'll bark at you and push against you until you do," Cheri says. "When the line bends, he's up right away and following that movement in the water."

It's not a food thing. Sure Rob Dog gets his own stringer, but he never eats the prize. "The first fish is always his," Cheri says. "He just makes sure it's on shore and it can't swim away."

Living in northwest Arkansas, they frequently fish for trout in the White River about a half-hour from their home, sometimes for the day or camping overnight. "We don't do any other vacations, unless we can take the dogs," Cheri says. They've added two more pups to their brood since getting Rob. "We have a tent trailer, and we'll take it out and clean it up and restock. If we put it back in the garage and don't hook it up to the van, Robby will pout for three days."

Dog-Friendly Lodgings and Attractions

Why not let a dog-friendly destination inspire an itinerary? With so many lodges, inns, B&Bs, and hotels dedicated to pooch pleasures, it is easy to create a holiday for the entire multispecies pack. Check out one of many dog-centered travel books (such as *Traveling with Your Pet: The AAA Pet Book* or a regional guide) or online listings (including *www.fidofriendly.com, www.bringyourpet.com, www.petswelcome.com,* and *www.dogfriendly.com*) to get started.

Don't confuse "dog-tolerant" with "dog-friendly." Not all "dog-friendly" accommodations are friendly in the same degree, and differences in degree can make or break your vacation. Mitch Frankenberg, owner of the Paw House Inn (see "Dream Job: Dog-Friendly Innkeepers"), encourages travelers to ask questions about dog-oriented amenities. It's up to you to determine if the place you are headed is merely dog tolerant. It's especially helpful to ask what guests traveling without dogs will be expecting. There are winter nights at the Paw House Inn when guests relaxing around the living room fire are joined by more than a dozen sleeping pups. Sounds like heaven, or hell, depending on your drool threshold.

COAXING A RELUCTANT DOG TO SWIM

Not all dogs swim. Some reluctant dogs remain reluctant and never take the plunge. But it's great low-impact exercise, and good for rinsing off and cooling down, so here are some tested strategies.

- *Try floating food.* When retrieving sticks and balls won't work, toss treats into the water for the food-motivated. Just be sure the treats don't sink too quickly.

- *Jump in yourself.* Sally Oien swims long distances in Seattle's Lake Washington and tried for years to get her dog, Gus, to join her. After a couple seasons watching Sally intently from the beach, Gus swam out. She's been Sally's swimming buddy ever since. Be warned, though: Paddling dogs can be a hazard when they try to climb onto you in open water. A veterinary surgeon in Portland lost her bikini top to an overzealous Lab–terrier mix.

- *Use a leash.* Pennsylvanian Kevin Meese created a mega-leash by hooking three six-foot leashes together and attaching it to the collar of his swimming-averse dog. Then he hopped into the family pool with the other end of the leash and called Country, his greyhound mix. Country is so well leash trained, he overcame his antipathy for water and jumped into the pool to reach Kevin. Unfortunately, he tried to run in the water, splashing awkwardly with his front legs. "I would hold him under his belly and walk him around the pool so he got the idea of letting his body lie flat and pulling with his legs to really swim," says Kevin, about a technique you see parents use with children (usually sans leash). "Now, Country loves the water so much, he will just run up to the pool and jump in to cool off on his own." Greyhounds aren't known for their passion for water, but Kevin has trained three more to love it. And Country has distinguished himself with a slew of DockDog world records.

Learn about running a dog-friendly establishment through a Vocation Vacations mentorship at the Paw House Inn. (See "Canine Careers," in the "At the Park" chapter.)

"Dog camps" don't necessarily mean there will be actual camping. Mountain Betties have been disappointed to discover that camp can sometimes be a euphemism. If you want a backpacking experience, this may not be your best bet.

Set a good example.

If you're staying in a hotel, a motel, cabins, or a lodge where dogs are tolerated rather than celebrated, be extra conscientious:

- Bring supplies so you can clean up any accidents. If you have a heavy shedder and plan to stay a few days, a hand vac or a rotating brush sweeper wouldn't be out of the question.
- Walk through hotel hallways quietly. A rubber band or tape wrapped around dog tags quiets jingling.
- Ask for a room on the ground floor, so the heavy paw steps or leaps off the bed don't disturb folks in the room below.

Ask the right questions.

How much for the dog? Even at pet-friendly hotels, the cost of a dog isn't always included and can vary greatly. Also, ask if there are any restrictions on the weight, breed, or number of dogs permitted.

A VACATION FOR, NOT JUST WITH, DOGS

During her first-ever trip to the Caribbean, Mary Kate McDermott had lunch every day with a black-and-white goat. While most vacationers were snorkeling or slathering on extra layers of sunscreen, Mary Kate was bottle feeding Little Black Magic, who had been paralyzed in a fall and separated from her mother.

An experienced groomer from Edmonds, Washington, Mary Kate spent three weeks on St. Martin, volunteering at the only private animal shelter on the island. She had never done volunteer work, but when she learned about the opportunity to put her professional skills to good use—and see a bit more of the world—she leaped.

Like the booming field of eco-tourism, combining a vacation with good works is becoming more common, especially among dog people. Raising and caring for a dog is an initiation into the reality that not all dogs are as happy or healthy as our own. That knowledge often inspires people to volunteer, and because time can be at a premium, some wannabe do-gooders combine a vacation with work at a shelter, sanctuary, or spay-neuter clinic.

Mary Kate paid for her own travel and food and received free room and use of a car. She worked almost every day, and the days were long. The biggest challenge was ticks. Because there was no money for tick-repellent treatments, Mary Kate spent much of her time pulling engorged ticks out of the ears and noses of unhappy strays. She barely saw the beach. A year later, she returned for a second volunteer mission.

But Mary Kate's story doesn't end there. When the shelter ran into financial trouble, St. Martin officials stepped in to close it. Part-time island resident and full-time dog lover Audrey Waldron heard about the closure. She commandeered three cargo vans and in under an hour pulled out as many dogs as possible—fifty in all—before officials shut everything down and euthanized the resident dogs. She brought them all back to her villa on four acres.

"That's when I got the call. Out of the blue," Mary Kate remembers. "Audrey said, 'You don't know me but I heard from friends on the island that you'd take some dogs.' I just said 'Sure.'"

In batches of four to six puppies, Mary Kate found homes for the shelter refugees through friends, family, and clients at her Seattle dog day-care business. The dogs were often malnourished and sometimes recovering from mange and parvo, an intestinal virus. She was one of several individuals in various parts of the country to help place the dogs in homes in the United States and Canada.

Today, Mary Kate continues to be a key player in the Animal Rescue League, teaming up with Audrey and St. Martin resident Shelley Crane to find homes for new strays, including puppies found dumped in back alleys and garbage bins.

"It has transformed everything," she says. "It's all I think about."

Dog Camps

Dog Camps are springing up around the country. I'm not talking about places you send your dogs for a few weeks of weight loss and mournful letters home. These are camps designed for dogs and their bipeds, where you participate in dog-centered activities together such as agility, freestyle dance, clicker training, carting, dock diving, dog fur spinning, tracking, Frisbee, and on

Sanctuaries, reserves, clinics, and shelters around the world offer opportunities for organized or informal volunteer vacations. To find an organization in a destination you plan to visit, go to *www.greenpeople.org*.

You can buy a preloaded pet first-aid kit or make one yourself. Lizzi created her own after consulting her vet and the book *Emergency First Aid for Your Dog* by Tamara S. Shearer, DVM. She also found ideas by looking at first-aid kits available online.

Lizzi keeps her dogs' regular collars dry to avoid contributing to hot spots or fungal issues. Her swimming collars are neon orange, soft plastic that don't soak up water, the sort that are traditionally used for hunting dogs.

and on. From Maian Meadows (*www.maianmeadows.com*) in Gig Harbor, Washington, and Camp Winnaribbun (*www.campw .com*) on Lake Tahoe to Barking Hills Country Club (*www.barkinghills.com*) in Lebanon, New Jersey, and Camp Dog Wood North (*www.campdogwoodnorth.com*) in Ontario, Canada, camps are also swell places to meet other dog enthusiasts.

DOG-GONE PACKING LIST

Lizzi Kadow in Chicago loves hitting the open road with her golden retriever, Ginger. More recently they have been joined by her rat terrier, Pooch. They've seen Niagara Falls, the summit of Whiteface Mountain in the Adirondacks, Wisconsin lakes, the Smoky Mountains in Tennessee, and even Dog Scout Camp in Michigan, plus New York City, Minnesota, Iowa, Kentucky, and Pennsylvania.

Like many dog-loving wanderers, Lizzi enjoys collecting and sharing road-tested wisdom. Below is her master packing list, along with some additional suggestions from other veteran canine-toting road warriors. Don't be overwhelmed. This isn't intended as a must-bring list but a could-bring list, depending on where you are traveling.

General Gear
- First-aid kit
- Pick-up bags
- Leashes

- Extra leash
- Swimming collar
- Life vest
- ID cape
- Reflective vests
- Collar light, such as a Puplight
- Flashlight
- Collapsible exercise pen, crate, or tie-out
- Local reference card

Food/Water
- Dog food and bottled water
- Health supplements
- Treats, chewies, bones
- Food and water bowls
- Extra bowls
- Travel calmer herbal supplement for anxious dogs

Other Equipment
- Dog backpacks
- Mat or bed for destination
- Sheets to cover furniture or beds

ID capes are small vests often worn by assistance dogs. "If Ginger was ever lost, her cape also serves as a very visible sign that this dog is not a stray or homeless dog but is lost," Lizzi says. "Ginger's cape also has a patch on one side that reads, 'Ask to pet me, I'm friendly,' which is helpful when we are out at festivals or other events."

Lizzi creates a reference card for her own use, with veterinarian contacts near her destination.

Don't forget a spoon and pop-tops for canned food.

Michelle Goodman's dog, Buddy, tends to pace and bark at a new place. At one cabin, the Seattleite discovered towels piled into a bed helped calm him down. Now she always brings his bed for physical and emotional comfort. She also wears him out with play during the day and avoids duplex cabins just in case.

Even at dog-friendly destinations, you want to keep fur off bed covers and furniture.

You may not plan to bathe your dog, but he may have other plans. There is a lot of stinky stuff on life's highway. Be prepared to wash it off.

Old-time chill pill: Martha E. lives on the Mississippi Gulf Coast, just a couple blocks from the water in an area greatly affected by Hurricane Katrina. "After Katrina, it was so hot!" she says. She bought some screw-top cloth ice bags, which she filled and put on the heads and necks of her dogs, Harley and Hershey. "They loved that and it helped keep them cool."

- Booties
- Coat
- Towels
- Blanket to cover car seats
- Toys
- Fanny pack to carry treats and baggies

Grooming Supplies
- Grooming spray, waterless shampoo, shampoo
- Brush and flea comb
- Pet wipes
- Lint rollers

Hot Weather Extras
- Cooling crate fan
- Cooling coats or wraps
- Freezable dog bowl
- Dog-safe sunscreen

Documentation
- Vaccination records
- Health certificate (if you're traveling out of the country)

DREAM JOB: DOG-FRIENDLY INNKEEPERS

Jen Fredreck and Mitch Frankenberg used to travel all the time with their two big Labs, Mario, who is black, and Shakespeare, who is yellow. "We were never satisfied with the places we stayed," Mitch says. "They weren't welcoming."

So six years ago they decided to do something about it. Jen was an attorney working at a law school and Mitch was a financial analyst. They traded in their fast-track New York existence and opened the Paw House Inn in West Rutland, Vermont. Mitch took an online innkeeper class, but mostly they learned the business through trial and error.

Today, the 1786 farmhouse near Killington and Okemo ski areas includes eight dog-ready rooms (with twenty more on the way), an on-site dog sitter, and training classes. A 5,000-square-foot facility with training, grooming, agility, day care, and dog-friendly restaurant is under construction. Dogs are welcome everywhere in the surprisingly fur- and dander-free environment. And there are a lot of small touches—dog-themed movies and art, dog beds in every room, and homemade dog treats.

"It's not the glorified, romantic ideal," Jen admits. "Until you actually own an inn, you're not going to know what it's like. The overriding theme is hard work and plenty of it."

Still, there are times when she'll be out in the snow playing with the dogs, her husband, and sons, Drew and Kyle, and she'll pause to appreciate the special life she's been able to create. "It's a fantastic family business," she says.

Pet Resume

Lizzi got the idea to create a resume for Ginger from members of Dogster.com, who used it to find a pet-friendly apartment. When she is reserving a cabin or cottage, she sends along Ginger's resume to reassure the owners that her dog is well behaved and well trained. Using the resume format that came with her computer's software, Lizzi simply modified the headers to be more dog oriented. In addition to Ginger's adorable mug and Lizzi's contact information, she includes a description of Ginger's physical appearance, personality, travel experience, work as a therapy dog, testing, qualifications (such as Canine Good Citizen), training, health and grooming history, and special skills. Under references, she includes Ginger's vet and her day-care manager.

Tip for apartment hunters: Improve your chances to land a pet-friendly apartment with a pet resume. A canine CV should include information a landlord will want to know, such as a description of your dog's personality, health and grooming history, and any special training. Also, collect letters of reference from your vet, dog walker, or trainer.

CAR SMARTS

While nose prints on the windows, a "Dog is my copilot" bumper sticker, and a thin blanket of fur aren't essential features of the true dogmobile, there are a few necessities according to dog-savvy travelers.

You always want a reliable way to temporarily secure your dog in some place other than a hot car.

What's in the well-equipped dogmobile?

- *Water bowl and water.* There are plenty of fancy no-spill water bowls available for the back of the car. But

Consider a collapsible bowl for outings and a spill-proof version for the car.

In case of an injury, a blanket can be used to carry a hurt pet or to keep him warm in case of shock. Extra blankets are a boon in a cold-weather breakdown.

Beloved dogmobile design extras include roomy cargo holds for crates, rubber or plastic floor mats, cup holders positioned far from wandering paws, and low-rise doors for easy entry and exit.

Tow tip: If you have to call for a tow truck, ask if dogs are allowed to ride with you.

don't let a trip to the doggie boutique slow you down. Toss a plastic bowl or recycled yogurt tub in the back of your car so you always have an easy drinking option for your dogs. Some pets won't drink water from vicinities that are foreign to them, so consider packing water from home.

- *A plastic bag dispenser.* Not only will you never go without but you also might be able to help a bag-less fellow dog walker.
- *Lint brush or roller.*
- *Medical/vaccination records.* In addition to a pet first-aid kit, some dog owners keep a copy of their dogs' medical and vaccination records in the car—in a folder titled "Open in Emergency."

Be selective about potty stops.

When you stop for a pee break in a new region, beware, especially at night! At the end of a drive from Orlando to his new home in Phoenix, Allen Kimble's dog, Vinny the Pug, discovered, much to his unpleasant surprise, that peeing on a cactus smarts. (Same with hot black top. If you can't hold your hand on the pavement for fifteen seconds, it's probably too hot for your dog.)

Preparations for your dog have a way of helping others. Mandy Hall of McKinney, Texas, carries extra leashes in her car. She's used them more than once to retrieve a stray. Slip or rope leashes are the most useful. The only time Mandy needed her pet first-aid kit (an idea that came from the travel safety badge she and her dog earned in Dog Scouts of America) was when she arrived on the heels of a car accident. While she waited for an ambulance, she applied sterile gauze to a woman's head wound.

Give your car a shave.

Martha E.'s dogs, Harley and Hershey, love road trips from their home in Mississippi to Gatlinburg. When she asks Harley if he wants to go to Tennessee, he grabs "his suitcase," a duffel bag for dog belongings. Unfortunately, during the ten-hour drive, the rottweiler–Australian shepherd and Akita–Labrador retriever leave a mass of fur in their wake. By the time they land, Martha says, "The PT Cruiser convertible looks like it has grown its own coat of hair."

She uses baby wipes to collect the vast majority of the fur, and a lint roller to pick up the rest. (Once back at home, she shop vacs the car floor.) It doesn't get up 100 percent of the fur, but enough. She says it's more effective and much less expensive than paying to have the car detailed.

Lizzi Kadow amps up the sticking power of the lint brush by using duct tape. She says it works better than a tape roller or a vacuum in pulling her terrier's hair from the upholstery weave of her car seats. Leather upholstery, on the other hand, makes sweeping away fur a breeze.

Spot the dismount.

Many auto-related injuries happen when the car isn't even moving. Lots of jumping from car seats onto pavement is tough on joints. Alan Bauer, a photographer for dog-friendly hiking books, has kicked up dust on more than a hundred different trails in Washington, Oregon, and Idaho, and logged 8,800 road miles with his dog, Mittens. He always lifts her out of the truck—and she waits for it—so she won't injure herself jumping down. In return, she's great company. Bauer says, "She never talks back to me and never complains about my driving."

If you're not that chivalrous or strong, there are ramps for cars to make the transition easier.

Take baby drives for motion sickness.

Despite Mittens's high pawdometer, she wasn't always this car-friendly. From the day they drove her home from the shelter, the black Border collie–Lab mix suffered nearly debilitating car sickness.

"I thought, I don't know how we are going to do this," Alan says. So he took Mittens on very short trips. "She'd be in the car six or seven times a day, but only for a few minutes each

Martha from Mississippi tackled Hershey's fear of cars by driving the dog to a fast-food joint for a hamburger. Hershey sat in Martha's lap and ate a kiddy burger with water. (No milkshake.) She was fine ever after.

time. When she'd get somewhere, she'd get out and we'd say 'Good job, good job,' and play for a bit."

A year of patience—and lots of two- to three-mile trips capped with treats and games and praise—turned things around. Once Mittens realized she'd be a dog model and trail tester on as many as three hikes a day, she learned to love the open road.

Other people report starting with even smaller steps, such as just sitting in the car with the engine off—followed by rewards.

TRIED-IT-MYSELF PRODUCT REVIEWS

One of the great things about dog people on the Internet is the opportunity to pool and share experiences. Many regular Joes become defacto experts in certain aspects of dog care because it's how they spend their time. Sometimes that knowledge translates into no-nonsense, TIM (tried-it-myself) product reviews posted on blogs, listservs, and websites.

Take Chris Crawford, a medic in the Army Reserve. A few years ago, she adopted a German shepherd, Abby K9, from a rescue. Chris does lots of activities in and around her Virginia home with Abby and became interested when her dog seemed to overheat. "I was surprised at just how fast her temperature rose," Chris says. She began monitoring Abby's temperature and evaluating the effectiveness of cooling products such as bandanas and cooling vests. She posted her uncompensated product reviews and a backgrounder on heatstroke on her website, *www. abbyk9.blogspot.com*. So now anyone can learn from her experiences.

Put the brakes on barking in the car.
Jose Pico's foster dog, Xena, barks on the drives to and from Best Friends Animal Society in Kanab, Utah, where he works and she spends days. He found that covering her crate with a blanket to block out stimulation (but not cut off ventilation) made a big difference.

Addressing a bad habit like barking in the car is difficult since you can't give your dog your full attention at the same time you are driving. If you want to work on correcting the behavior, ask someone else to do the driving, while you work with the dog.

Buckle Up

You wouldn't expect a child to travel without a car seat, so why let your dog face the same risks without protection? Ever since a seatbelt harness saved her dog Byron's life (see "Why Secure Your Dog"), Floridian Michelle Gonsalves has been a tireless advocate for securing pets while they travel in cars. She has researched crates and harnesses and now shares her experience and knowledge with others.

Crate your mate.
The American Kennel Club recommends crates, which not only secure your pet but also make removing a frightened and potentially aggressive pup from an accident safer for emergency personnel. The crate has to be sturdy like those approved for airlines. It also has to be small. If not, the dog moves around inside the crate in an accident or hard stop and can be hurt. Some people pad the inside of the crate to minimize this sort of injury.

A crate must also be tied down so it will not move in

Some road warriors swear that a few saltines on an otherwise empty stomach will calm a dog's car wobblies.

The stress of a long drive can be tough on dogs' tummies. Ask your vet about giving your pet a dose of medicine for upset stomachs, such as Pepto-Bismol, after a road trip, to keep middle-of-the-night bathroom breaks to a minimum.

With or without a crate, never place your dog in the front seat where an airbag can crush him or her.

If your dog is not in a crate or wearing a restraint, be doubly sure to lock car doors and electric window controls.

On Byron's harness is a note: "Do not take this dog out of this harness. He is very fast and you will not be able to catch him."

an accident. The best method is to secure a line over and through the air holes of the crate and attach that line to the frame of the car.

Harness your load.

Crash-tested or high-tensile-strength harnesses can be attached to a seatbelt or child-seat LATCH system (see your car manual) as a dog restraint. The problem with a harness is that "most people who use one do not use it appropriately," Michelle says. It's too loose or tethered to the seat belt when the seat belt is not ratcheted into the locked position.

She recommends Ruff Rider Roadie vehicle restraints or the Champion Canine Seatbelt System (which Byron uses). For a less expensive solution, she recommends the Four-Paws safety harness (Byron's old harness). "That's the only other car harness I recommend because I crash tested it myself," she says.

Keep in mind, harnesses can break bones and cause injuries similar to those caused by seatbelts. Also, an upset dog in a harness can distract rescue personnel.

WHY SECURE YOUR DOG

On a spring day in 2005, Michelle Gonsalves was driving from Miami, where she was a graduate bio-medical science student, to her parents' home in Key Largo when she noticed the seatbelt harness on her one-year-old Italian greyhound, Byron, was loose.

"I thought, 'That's not right. I have to fix it,'" Michelle says. "And I did something that I never really do." She stopped on the side of the highway, moved Byron to the backseat, and tightened his harness and restraint. "Because I did that, I saved his life."

A half hour farther down the dangerous two-lane stretch through the Everglades, the car in front of Michelle's came to a sudden stop. She swerved to avoid a rear-end collision, but lost control on gravel and swung back into oncoming traffic. An SUV ran head-on into her.

Michelle broke her neck, both knees, her foot, and her sternum, damaged her liver and spleen, and shattered her ankle. When the paramedics arrived, she kept saying: "My dog's in the back. My dog's in the back. Can you see my dog?" Because the back seat had buckled under the weight of a box of dishes in her trunk, her rescuers couldn't see Byron at first. Michelle wouldn't be calmed until they found her thirteen-pound red-and-white show dog under the crumpled back seat—badly bruised and frightened but otherwise unhurt.

After she was airlifted to the hospital, a paramedic took Byron to a nearby animal shelter, where her father collected him. During the six weeks Michelle was in the hospital and for a while after, Byron went to live with his breeder, Lynn Hunt Hoffman. Lynn helped Byron overcome his new fear of cars. And because she knew Michelle would have mobility and access problems, Lynn trained him as a service dog. He learned how to work around the wheelchair Michelle needed for many months, how to turn on lights in dark rooms, retrieve dropped objects, help make the bed, and assist with laundry. (In addition, he also knows how to remove Michelle's shoes and socks—which is actually a trick he learned before the accident.)

During her recuperation, Michelle returned to the show ring with Bryon, handling him from a wheelchair. Almost exactly one year after the accident, they won his championship. Michelle says, "The entire ringside erupted because everybody knew."

Because of her experience, Michelle is a big believer in restraining dogs in cars, and she's spent a lot of time learning what's best. She recommends using either crates or a high-tensile or crash-tested harness restraint. Neither is perfect but both are better than nothing.

DOGS ON A PLANE—TIPS, NOT A MOVIE

Not all dog travel is by car, of course. More and more dogs are earning frequent flier miles. (I mean that purely metaphorically, but you never know.) Barbara DeBry is the go-to tipster for flying with dogs. As the owner of Puppy Travel in Utah, she arranges flights for dogs with places to go.

Don't sedate your dog. Many airlines won't accept a dog they know has been sedated.

Put your pup first.

Barbara says if your dog will be flying in the baggage compartment, don't buy your airplane ticket *before* planning for him or her. Issues such as airline-specific weather restrictions on transporting pets can create headaches during very hot and very cold seasons. Plus something as simple as a large dog crate that won't fit on all planes, for example, can put the kibosh on a journey at the last minute.

Get the right kind of crate.

Buy an airline-approved crate. The number-one complication with shipping pets is escape. A collapsed crate can injure or free your frightened pet. Barbara also suggests fastening the crate door with a plastic zip tie, so curious handlers don't accidentally free your pup.

DREAM JOB: TRAVEL AGENT TO THE DOGS

Oodles the schnoodle doesn't like to fly. Since most dogs never get within tire-biting distance of an airplane, that hardly sounds like a crisis. But the four-year-old schnauzer–poodle mix isn't any dog. She's the inspiration for Puppy Travel, a companion-animal travel agency in Utah, which may have been the first of its kind.

Oodles's guardian, company founder Barbara DeBry, specialized in traditional travel for more than twenty years—working for airlines, a travel agency, and travel departments at large corporations. Like a dog dropping a juicy bone in her lap, Oodles entered her life at the moment she needed an angle for launching her own travel business.

Since 2003, Barbara has helped countless breeders transport puppies, families relocate furry siblings, and travelers realize canine-friendly holidays or business trips around the country and in Asia, Europe, South America, Canada, Mexico, and Africa.

"It's something you can't do over the Internet," says Barbara, who knows which airlines deliver the best service for pets. Not only are regulations frequently changing, but also the unique requirements of pet travel demand hands-on problem solving. Connections between airlines with different policies can be a boondoggle. Immigration rules are complicated and reservation agents often don't know what's what when it comes to these rarer cases. For travelers who don't understand how the system works, it can be surprisingly expensive.

Even though it's her bread and butter, Barbara sometimes dissuades her clients from taking a dog along. Business trips or short transcontinental or international vacations may not be in a dog's best interest. She says, "Begin by asking yourself: Is it worth it?"

Although the business is called Puppy Travel, Barbara has arranged flights for parrots, turtles, rabbits, chinchillas, and other animals. Cats are her favorite. "They travel great," Barbara says. "They just go in their zone." High praise that has to annoy the travel-sensitive Oodles a little bit.

Keep tabs on your pooch.
Ask the flight attendant to check if your dog is onboard. Animals are the last on and the first off, so it may take awhile, but usually airline personnel are more than happy to determine when your dog is safely aboard.

Make your dog's flight a pleasant one.
If you're planning on bringing a dog in a carry-on bag, Barbara says, be hands-on. Ask security personnel if you can take your dog out of the carrier during security checks. Walk your dog in the terminal—dogs will fly better if they get to stretch their legs while they wait. Have supplies handy to clean up any dog mess. It's a little like traveling with children. You have to be ready for any eventuality.

Transfer at pet-friendly airports.
More and more airports have dog-friendly pit stops. The Sky Harbor International Airport in Phoenix boasts two pet parks, the Bone Yard and the Paw Pad Pet Park, with clean-up mitts and fresh water. There are animal-relief stations/pet-exercise areas with varying degrees of space and comfort at Los Angeles International Airport, San Diego International, Denver International, Minneapolis-St. Paul International, Reno-Tahoe International, Port Columbus International, Portland International, Austin-Bergstrom International, Seattle's Sea-Tac International, and others.

Mind the culture gap.

People don't feel the same way about dogs in different parts of the country and even more so around the world. In Paris, a dog might sit in your lap at a restaurant; in other cities, a dog might be in the soup. If you plan to take your dog to a foreign country, learn a little about local attitudes.

When Alisa Puga-Keesey moved to Uganda to do development work, her constant companion was a Rhodesian ridgeback named Scout. It wasn't easy at first; the locals didn't get it. "Culturally, they don't treat animals the way we do," Alisa says. But because of their relationship with her and Scout's charm, they began to accept him.

Still, when her butcher discovered she was feeding cubed goat meat to her dog, he came after her with a machete. A machete! "I said, 'Hey, cultural sensitivity is a two-way street.'" Alisa remembers telling the butcher that Scout was her *askari*, a personal guard like those that many people in Uganda keep. "'An *askari* costs fifty shillings a month. He is our *askari* and it costs that much to feed him.'" The man understood that logic and told her she got the better deal since "*askaris* fall asleep at night and that dog probably doesn't."

TRAVEL BUGS

Mandy Hall takes her Great Dane, Simon, on geocaching adventures in her home state of Texas and beyond. Geocaching is the hobby of using a Global Positioning System and online coordinates to find hidden caches (often a log book and trinkets) and hiding caches for others. Simon has his own online geocaching account, tracking gear, and goodies to leave behind. He also has a Travel Bug.

Travel Bugs are tags with unique tracking numbers. Usually, they are moved from cache to cache. The fun is in tracking the Bug's journey around the state, the country, maybe even the world. In Simon's case, he *is* the Travel Bug. After meeting him on the trail or at geocaching events, fellow treasure hunters enter notes about these experiences and even pictures of their meeting. His Travel Bug account becomes a high-tech travelogue. (To learn more about Travel Bugs, visit www.geocaching.com/track/travelbugs.aspx.)

Adopt on the road.

San Diego resident Daiva Gedgaudas frequently travels with her husband and children to Mexico's Baja Peninsula, where she sees lots of emaciated, mangy strays. Rather than wringing her hands over the sight, she took action. She connected with the Baja Animal Sanctuary, the only no-kill shelter in northern Mexico, located about twenty-five miles south of the San Ysidro border. Through the sanctuary, Daiva adopted Alley, a malnourished eight-month-old puppy named for the alley where she was found. The sanctuary managed all the details of customs, but also required San Diego volunteers to conduct two home visits.

More than a year later, the blonde German shepherd mix with a dark muzzle has filled out and her coat shines. The only signs of her early days are pockmarked teeth, which the vet attributes to a bout with parvovirus when she was young, and timidity around unfamiliar people. Daiva continues to support the work of the Baja Animal Sanctuary by telling Alley's story to anyone who will listen and with contributions.

Fonts of Wisdom: Dog Park Brain Trust

A LITTLE MORE ABOUT *DOG PARK WISDOM* TIPSTERS (in alphabetical order by first name).

Aaron Wiehe lives and skateboards with his husky, Nisha, in Seattle, Washington.

Nature photographer **Alan Bauer** of Fall City, Washington, rarely hikes alone. Always nearby is Mittens, a black Border collie mix with a white bib and socks . . . I mean, mittens.

The shea butter products Santa Cruz resident **Alisa Puga-Keesey** first created for her Rhodesian ridgeback, Scout, might now be used to help people.

Sixteen pounds of pure power, Vinny the Pug is trying to set a world record for climbing boulders in and around his Phoenix, Arizona, home. At the other end of the leash is his trainer, photographer, publicist and biographer **Allen Kimble**.

Amanda Tikkanen has hiked at least 500 miles, mostly in and around Indiana where she lives, with her Louisiana catahoula leopard dog, Beau.

King is just one of **Amy Lerma**'s four dogs. His days in Cornersville, Tennessee, are filled with games of tug-of-war and keep-away, herding his pack mates, cooling off in a plastic pool, and chomping a plush carrot that grunts.

Anne Croghan lives with two big-eared, sniff-happy beagles, Amos and Oliver, in Seattle.

Anne Henshaw first saw Mia outside her casita in Mexico, where the three-month-old puppy with mange was defending an empty chip bag. It took four months to get her healthy enough to travel to Alaska, where Anne lives part-time.

In the woods outside Fairbanks, Alaska, **Arna Dan Isacsson** shares her cabin and fourteen acres with more than twenty formerly abandoned, neglected sled dogs.

What's a book of down-home advice without some words of wisdom from a mother-in-law? Mine, **Audrey Fischer**, has lived with and puppy-loved Ernie, Rusty, and Minnie.

Although **Barbara DeBry**'s schnauzer–poodle, Oodles, doesn't like to fly, her second schnoodle, Soozie, is a mellow traveling companion, which is good news for the owner of Puppy Travel, the Utah-based animal travel and transport company.

Barbara Teigen lives with Master Earthdog, Eugene U Genius, and several other dachshund buddies in Nashotah, Wisconsin.

Bev Sparks lives with and photographs her dogs—Benny Capra, a thirteen-year-old white shepherd–husky–Lab mix, and Eddie, a two-year-old pointer mix (our cover dog!)—in south Seattle.

Brenda Bryan teaches traditional yoga and yoga with dogs in the Seattle area. She also blogs (*www.dogyoga.blogspot.com*) and is writing a book about yoga with dogs.

A cross between a bear and a deer—that's how **Brian** and **Val Bate** of Portland, Oregon, describe their dog, Hank, a.k.a., Henry Wilson Bartholomew Bridges Bate, Herder of Goats, Flusher of Grouse, Earl of Long Tongue.

Inspired by her dog, Miguel Raoul, elementary school teacher **Briana Solovitz** made pugs a motif in her O'Fallon, Missouri, classroom.

Caitlin lives in Kitchener, Ontario, with her pug–Chihuahua, Bailey; Himalayan Siamese cat, Muffin; and bunny, Alice.

Now based in Placerville, California, **Carol Beebee**, formerly a travel nurse, spent years touring the country and hiking rain forests, glaciers, and sand dunes with her photographer husband, Martin, and their golden retriever, Holly.

With a Border collie named Bob at her side, Portland, Oregon, resident **Carolyn Eddy** hikes with pack goats in the summer and writes about those adventures in the winter for *Goat Tracks Magazine*.

Carrie Comer's two-year-old son, PJ, takes care of their Brittany, Katie, by helping to feed her, dispensing treats during her bath time, reading to her, and playing with her during noisy Virginia storms.

Rob Dog joined **Cheri McDonald**'s family in northwest Arkansas six years ago. After Cheri's autistic son, Ryan, came out of his shell with a Frisbee-playing Border collie at the park, she decided to adopt one of their own.

Chris Crawford lives with and blogs about her German shepherd, Abby K9, in northern Virginia.

Christie Withers lives on Vashon Island in Washington's Puget Sound with two black poodles, an orange cat, my sister Hilary, and their son, Zander. Their big dog, Phoenix, has channeled the late Wizard's food-stealing ways.

Cindy Trimble Kelly, owner of Trimble Kelly Studios, Inc., lives with three corgis (Peanut, Bandita, and Lucy), three farm dogs (Sally, Bubba, and Tiger), three horses (Goldie Locks, Doc, and Traveler), and a spotted donkey named The General, on a farm in Blue Ridge, Georgia.

Claudine Randazzo lives with Bo and Chance, rescue pups, in Flagstaff, Arizona, where she is a writer who sometimes gets to review dog resorts.

In addition to his tick-removal strategy, Northern Californian **Cloude Porteus** has posted instructions for curing hiccups, opening a bottle of beer without a bottle opener, and making Bolognese sauce at Instructables.com.

Daiva Gedgaudas and her family enjoy walking the coast of Carlsbad, California, with their favorite companion, Alley (Alley Beans to the kids), each and every weekend.

Four dachshunds keep things interesting in the Seattle home of **Dani Baker** and **Mali McGolden**.

An economics researcher in Ames, Iowa, **Dave Swenson** has finished five marathons and one ultra-marathon with his rat terrier, Miss Daisy One Dot.

On a trip to Morocco, Seattle residents **Dean** and **Kathy Schultz** bought a hand-tooled leather bed for Omar, their French bulldog.

When **Detta Juusola** (*www.dettasspindle.com*) isn't spinning dog fur into yarn, she's hanging out with her three dogs, Sunny, Pluto, and Bonzai, or any one of her fourteen (that's not a typo) children in Maple Plain, Minnesota.

A Samoyed named Toby was Seattle-based dating expert and writer **Diane Mapes**'s first love. They grew up together on a strawberry farm.

In early 2007, **Doina Berndt** adopted a Whippet puppy named Whisper, who had been abused and then dumped at a shelter in Oklahoma. He was helped in adjusting to his new life by his best friend, Maya, a Lurcher Doina had rescued a few years earlier.

My sister **Eileen Wogan** lives with two cats in Goleta, California, and is a volunteer dog walker for her local animal shelter and for neighbors.

Garrett Rosso, co-chair of NYCdog Dog Park Committee and manager of the Tompkins Park dog run in Manhattan, lives in the East Village with two Rhodesian ridgebacks and a corgi–Jack Russell mix.

A serious allergy to flea bites made **Gayle Kirschenbaum**'s life a dog-free zone for many years. But when the New York City filmmaker met a shih tzu named Chelsea, all bets were off. (Learn more about Chelsea's big screen debut at *www.dogamentary.org*.)

Geri Sim and Katie, a peanut-butter loving Sheltie, spend long hours in their New Hyde Park, New York, kitchen, fine-tuning dog-biscuit and cake recipes for the Honeybark Bakery (*www.honeybark.com*).

When **George Gadda**'s Akita went blind at the age of three, neither man nor dog broke stride. The Bay Area resident and owner of Tidy Turf Pet Waste Removal Service (*www.tidyturf .com*) was in it for the long haul. He waited and watched as Pacino adapted, learning how to walk off-leash, and run and play despite his disability.

Haley Poulos day hikes and backpacks with her catahoula leopard dog mix, Charlotte, in the Cascade Mountains not far from her home in Silverdale, Washington. On a recent trek they ran out of water, but her resourceful sidekick found a full bottle trailside.

Although she spends her days at a zoo in Seattle, **Helen Shewman** shares her home with four dogs and three cats.

Seattle-based dog photographer and pet portrait artist **Jamie Pflughoeft** (*www.cowbelly .com*) was surprised and thrilled to discover she could make a living hanging out with dogs.

Jeanne Modesitt, a children's book writer in Kanab, Utah, spends many mornings walking dogs at Best Friends Animal Society and afternoons at home with her rescued eighteen-year-old Westie–corgi mix, Katie.

When **Jeff Jablow** of Round Rock, Texas, first spied Nick, a golden retriever–standard poodle mix, the eight-week-old puppy was chewing bark off a tree. Today, the pooch prefers water, lots of it, and is a water rescue dog and a member of Dog Scouts.

No cats allowed at the Paw House Inn, **Jen Frederick** and **Mitch Frankenberg**'s dog-friendly retreat in Vermont's Green Mountain National Forest.

Since 1998, **Jim Greenway** has managed the Traildog group on Yahoo.com. He's currently without a trail pal (Shadow's successor, a Boston terrier named Molly, prefers the comforts of home). But as a Scoutmaster, he still hikes in northern Georgia with his son's troop.

Mellowing with age, a troublemaking rescue dog named Chester continues to challenge my cousin **Joanie Warner** and her husband **Bob Mahler**'s patience in Seattle, Washington.

Motivated by a dog who loved to munch on rocks, **Joe Markham** invented a little chew toy known as the Kong.

"Just do it"—that's what **Jose Pico** tells anyone thinking about volunteering to work with dogs. The volunteer-turned-employee at Best Friends Animal Society in Utah says, "the dogs are very grateful for everything you do for them."

Joshua Madsen is learning how to balance time and attention between his first dog, Tucker (a miniature schnauzer), and his new puppy, Tommy (an Australian shepherd), at home, in the park, and on the trails in Orlando, Florida.

Joyce Gehl's poodle, Rocky, was named after swallowing a rock, which had to be surgically removed, when he was only five weeks old. She now keeps his namesake in a jar in her West Seattle home.

Judy Trockel lives with her husband, Jim, and three pups—Boogie, P.D., and Brown

Dog—in Redmond, Washington, where she is a very active volunteer in SODA (Serve Our Dog Areas), which maintains an off-leash area that receives about 700,000 visits every year.

Jim and **Julie Dugan** are working hard to make Pierce County, Washington, a no-kill community, as they raise their daughter, Samantha, and two rescue dogs, Jack and Gracie.

In one year, **Justin Lichter** and his dog, Yoni, hiked 10,000 miles of trail in Mexico, the United States, and Canada, during which he wore through twenty-four pairs of shoes and she tore through about 700 pounds of food. When they aren't hiking, Justin and Yoni live in Truckee, California.

Gleason and Denali were not merely two wonderful husky mixes. As best buds of my editor **Kate Rogers**, they were also important inspirations for *Dog Park Wisdom*.

Ken Hoeve lives on a ranch in Gypsum, Colorado, with horses, cats, and four dogs, including a Chihuahua named Pee Wee. In 2007, the Crazy River Dog Contest in nearby Salida was so-named in memory of the late Jiggy Dawg, Ken's feisty brown pit bull who had no fear of rough water.

Country may be the reigning DockDog world champion, but he wasn't always a winner. The greyhound mix was given to Pennsylvanian **Kevin Meese** (who trained him to glory) after he had washed out in field-trial competition.

After three months in a shelter in Prescott, Arizona, Grizzley Ralph (a biscuit-loving chow chow mix) was rescued by **Kevin N.** and his girlfriend, **Lessie**. Eventually, they returned to the shelter and brought home a malamute–Lab pal named Abigail Grace.

As a production accountant for movies, **Kyle O'Brien-Hoving** is often out-of-town filming on location, so her husband, **John Hoving**, has had to master the solo technique of walking their three big golden retrievers in Manhattan, which means managing two energetic pups and one slowpoke.

After years visiting and volunteering at off-leash areas in the St. Paul area, **Laura Jean Rathmann** now attends playgroups with her golden retriever, Janna, who is in training for Helping Paws Service Dogs.

Linda Heidt says her four ferrets sleep about twenty hours a day in her home in Pensacola, Florida. But during the other four hours, they play chase with her dog, Scooby Doo, build nests, and steal shiny objects and remote controls.

More than half of **Lisa Port**'s clients have dogs, so the Seattle landscape designer (with two cats of her own) is always conjuring pet-friendly garden solutions.

Happy to share the joy of life with Ginger and Pooch, **Lizzi Kadow** created a free website (*www.chicagocanine.com*) loaded with Chicago-area canine information and activities, her travel packing list and product reviews of interest to dog folks everywhere.

For several years the challenges of caring for a partially paralyzed Newfoundland named Nell filled **Lynn T.**'s life with love and creativity.

Rascal (Border collie mix), Allie (Vizsla mix), and Simon (Great Dane) have kept Texas-resident **Mandy Hall** busy with everything from therapy work and obedience competitions to competitive Frisbee and geocaching.

Mark Ball, in Asheville, North Carolina, has trail dogs at both ends of the spectrum. His thirteen-year-old Australian shepherd, Dandee, has pretty much retired from hiking, while his two-year-old Hungarian Kuvasz, Riley, is a promising—if not entirely reliable—rookie.

Married with three young children and an aging dog, **Mark Peterson** still averages three days in the saddle, but most of his mountain-bike time these days happens in his office at the Kona Bicycle Company.

Martha E. weathered Hurricane Katrina in Ocean Springs, Mississippi, with her dogs, Harley and Hershey.

A critical care nurse in Durant, Oklahoma, **Mary "Mimi" Hill** always likes to have at least one resident weenie dog. That honor currently goes to Candy-O Cootinka.

Mary Martin bonded with her Australian shepherd, Keeper, in the agility ring. She lives with her husband, his agility dog, and another agility dog-in-training in eastern Washington State.

The most recent St. Martin stray to join **Mary Kate McDermott**'s pack is Joey, who was found tied to a tree. His collar had to be surgically removed and a bad break in his leg required amputation. But today in Edmonds, Washington, the honey-brown dog is just another happy-go-lucky hound.

During the season, **Mary Mischelle Kemp** takes Wednesdays off for trout fishing along Utah rivers with a pair of basset hounds.

Unhappy with the results of alpha training with past dogs, Boulder resident **Matt Cohn** has embraced positive reinforcement and the clicker method with two Lab mixes, Hazel and Rosie.

Matt Van Wormer is the cofounder of FIDOS (Friends Interested in Dogs and Open Space), an off-leash advocacy group in Boulder.

Variety is the spice of **Melanie B.**'s life in Alberta, Canada. She lives on a farm with eight cats and six dogs. Hank, Baba, and Buddy are her three Great Pyrenees; Taco is a German shepherd mix; Molly, a Border collie; and Lucy is a Chinese crested.

More than two years after a serious car accident, **Michelle Gonsalves** still has pain and trouble walking, but with Byron, an Italian greyhound service dog, at her side, the Miamian got her master's degree in biomedical science and is planning on attending medical school.

One of the reasons author **Michelle Goodman** fled the corporate life (an escape she describes in *The Anti 9-to-5 Guide*) was to spend more time with black Lab Buddy in her Seattle, Washington, home.

Nichole Royer's six dogs—three Alaskan malamutes, two Korean Jindos, and a Siberian husky—pull carts (rather than sleds) in the California desert. She's actively involved with Jindo rescue and frequently includes foster Jindos on her team.

When **Nicole Gendics** was a young girl, her father used to feed strays. Now she makes *him* crazy. She lives with seven dogs—including several with special needs—in Cleveland, Ohio.

Nora Boyd hikes and camps in Iowa with a Pembroke corgi, Gryphon, and a Nova Scotia duck-tolling retriever, Ranger.

When he's not fielding emails about his pet deskunking recipe or receiving toy skunks from family, **Paul Krebaum** is a consultant in polymer chemistry in Lisle, Illinois.

Even though she already had several dogs and cats, when **Peggy Sherman** discovered a severely dehydrated puppy with mange at the dump near her Florida home, she knew she had to save him. It's been a long but rewarding road with Rufus.

"When I work with dogs, the rest of the world is cut out," says **Peter Kunz**, who walks and trains dogs in New York City. "It makes me totally happy."

Petie Hoving lives on New York's Upper East Side with her two miniature pinschers. She started IMPS (Internet Miniature Pincher Service, *www.minpinrescue.org*) to improve the lives of homeless and abandoned min-pins through rescue, human care, and compassion.

The goofy antics of a chocolate Lab named Spencer inspired comic strip artist and South Carolina resident **Phil Juliano** to illustrate and write his first solo strip, *Best in Show*.

Renee Hensley lives in North Pole, Alaska, with Onyx, a black German shepherd who likes to decapitate squeaky toys.

Photographer **Robert Troup** lives with four Border collies, two mothers with a daughter each, in Boulder, Colorado.

Robin Haglund, the owner of Seattle landscape design company Garden Mentors, has lived with fifteen dogs of all breeds, ranging from unidentifiable mutts to show-quality Great Danes, including her current best friend, Shiloh, a Kerry beagle–terrier mix.

Soon after her honeymoon, **Sally Oien** dug up a year-old advertisement for Border collie puppies she'd filed away and called the number. Her timing was perfect. A new ad was going in the paper the very next day. Sally's pick of the litter was Gus.

Susan J. Hilger is the owner of S. J. Hilger Interiors in Charlotte, North Carolina, where she lives with her design muses Zach and Hannah, two rescue dogs. She also volunteers for Project Halo, supporting animal rescue in New Orleans after Hurricane Katrina.

Suzie deDisse has been a volunteer with the Evergreen Animal Protection League (EAPL) in Evergreen, Colorado, since its inception in 1981. She served as EAPL president for seventeen years. Suzie doesn't have any dogs, but she does have four cats.

Taresa D. recently added a greater Swiss mountain dog named Sabrina to her otherwise beagle-themed life in Seattle.

Tod Wohlfarth has made many new friends at the Leroy Dog Run in New York's Lower West Side.

Four standard poodles join **Vikki Kauffman** for outdoor adventures in the mountains near her Seattle, Washington, home.

"She's my number-one hobby," says Seattleite **Wendy Hughes-Jelen** about the shy Italian greyhound she adopted three years ago. From long walks to playgroups, Wendy says, "my life kind of revolves around her."

Whitney Wogan (yup, another sister) is a doting caretaker for two rescue dogs, Zipper and Zooma, in Boulder, Colorado.

Acknowledgments

THIS BOOK IS THE RESULT OF MANY HOURS spent in real and virtual dog parks, chatting with dedicated, inspiring, and generous dog people. Without their smarts, there would be no *Dog Park Wisdom*. Most of these folks are named in the pages of this book, but a few aren't mentioned directly. They gave their time and deserve their bones like everyone else. Thanks to Seattleites Janice Kajanoff, who makes to-die-for sportswear for sight hounds; Nancy Schutt, a painter who specializes in vibrant dog portraits; and Matt Warning, an economics professor whose trials with a deerhound named Fredi could be a book of its own. Also, thanks to dog group organizers Liz Carver in Brighton, Massachusetts; Shannon Sickmon in Atlanta; Rob Goddard in Toronto; and DeAnna Miller in St. Louis; who tapped their doggie connections for me.

I am indebted to Claudia Kawczynska, the editor of *Bark*, who gives me the always-welcome opportunity to write about the community of dog people for her fine magazine. Closer to home, I'm grateful to my co-collaborator, dog photographer Bev Sparks, who reminds me to follow my dog's lead into adventure. Also to my eagle-eyed friend, Carolyn Wennblom, who waded through these dog-laden pages just days after saying goodbye to the sweetest rottweiler a girl could want. And to my husband, Charlie, who always knows when I need a shoulder rub, a plate of pasta, or a wide berth.

Finally, thanks to Joan Gregory for minding the syntax, to Janet Kimball for managing the details, and to Kate Rogers at the Mountaineers Books and Skipstone, who conjured this book idea and then signed me up for the chance to realize it.

Index

About the Author
and the Photographer

WHEN SHE'S NOT WALKING, CUDDLING, furminating, feeding, or cajoling her dog Lulu, Lisa Wogan writes from her home in Seattle, Washington. While dogs are at the top of her topic list (she's the pets columnist for *NWSource.com* and a contributing editor for *The Bark* magazine), she also specializes in stories about people, home design, and any other oddball thing that comes her way for a variety of regional and national publications. You can contact Lisa and share with her your own tips for dog care at *www.dogparkwisdom.com.*

BEV SPARKS REGULARLY VISITS Seattle's dog parks with Benny, the Fun Police, and Eddie, the Humper. More of her work can be seen at *www.dogphotography.com*, as well as on greeting cards, magnets, and a variety of book covers.